Popular Mechanics

do-it-yourself encyclopedia

GUIDE TO

FAMILY

GARDENING

HEARST DIRECT BOOKS

NEW YORK

Acknowledgments

This book is published with the consent and cooperation of POPULAR MECHANICS Magazine

POPULAR MECHANICS Staff:

Editor-in-Chief: Joe Oldham
Managing Editor: Bill Hartford
Special Features Editor: Sheldon M. Gallager
Automotive Editor: Wade A. Hoyt
Home and Shop Editor: Steven Willson
Electronics/Photography Editor: Stephen A. Booth
Boating/Outdoors Editor: Joe Skorupa
Science Editor: Timothy H. Cole
Graphics Director: Bryan Canniff
Editorial Production: John Bostonian, Jr.

POPULAR MECHANICS **Guide to Family Gardening**

Editor: C. Edward Cavert
Written by: Don Geary
Manufacturing: Ron Schoenfeld
Graphic Enhancement: Thomas Dahlen
Technical Consultants:
    Wilma Cavert
    William Dare
    Barbara S. Hatheway
    Tim Snider
    Penelope Spangler
    Gretchen Taylor

Credits

Photographs reproduced with permission of:

W. Atlee Burpee Co, page 10 (left); page 102 (top left; top right; bottom right); page 103 (top left; bottom left); page 106 (center left); page 107 (top right); page 114 (bottom left); page 50 (bottom left); page 52 (bottom right); page 54 (bottom right; top right); page 56 (top left); page 57 (top right; bottom left); page 58 (top left; top right); page 60 (top right); page 61 (center left); page 62 (top left: bottom left; bottom right); page 63 (top left); page 65 (bottom left); page 73 (top right); page 74 (bottom left); page 80 (top left); page 81 (top left); page 92 (bottom left).

California Redwood Association, page 33; page 34.

Consep Mebranes, Inc., page 46 (top left).

Fiskars Manufacturing Co. page 18 (right).

Gardener's Supply Co., page 1 (lower right); page 2 (top left); page 28 (center left); page 29 (bottom right); page 3 (top left); page 30 (top right); page 4 (right); page 86 (top right).

W.W. Grinder Co., page 41 (bottom right).

Harris Moran Seed Company, page 105 (top left; bottom right); page 107 (bottom left); page 3 (center); page 31 (center right); page 49 (top right); page 5; page 51 (bottom right); page 52 (top left); page 53 (top right; bottom left; bottom right); page 54 (top left); page 60 (bottom right); page 61 (center right); page 63 (center and bottom); page 73 (bottom right); page 76 (bottom right); page 77 (center right); page 85 (top left).

Kemp Company, page 21 (left); page 40.

Koppers Company, Inc., page 2 (lower left); page 25 (bottom right); page 27 (center left); page 29 (bottom left); page 31 (bottom).

LaMotte Chemical Products Co., page 4 (left); page 36.

Lord & Burnham, page 1 (top); page 25 (top); page 30 (center left, bottom left and right).

Mantis Manufacturing Co., page 115 (center left); page 21 (right); page 23 (bottom right); page 41 (bottom left).

Natural Gardening Research Center, page 7 (top); page 23 (top left); page 43 (bottom right); page 45 (center right); page 60 (top left).

L.R. Nelson Corp., page 22 (bottom right).

Rodales Organic Gardening, page 13 (top).

Sears Roebuck & Co., page 19 (top right); page 20 (bottom left); page 20 (bottom right); page 22 (bottom left); page 43 (bottom left); page 85 (bottom right).

Vme Edom Smith Photos, Manassas, Virginia, page 11 (right); page 14 (top); page 8 (bottom left); page 9 (bottom right).

Charles Tack Photographer, Reston, Virginia, page 66; page 67; page 68; page 69 (top right); page 70; page 71 (top right); page 72.

Illustrations by:

Thomas Dahlen, page 3 (bottom right); page 8 (top right); page 9 (top left); page 10 (right); page 104 (bottom left); page 108 (top right); page 11 (left); page 12 (bottom); page 13 (bottom); page 14 (bottom); page 15 (bottom); page 19 (center right); page 19 (left); page 22 (top left); page 23 (top right); page 28 (bottom right); page 38; page 39; page 42; page 56 (top right); page 69 (top left); page 71 (top left); page 93 (bottom right).

Mary Lang, Illustrator, page 16 (top); page 26 (top and bottom); page 27 (top and bottom); page 28 (bottom left); page 29 (center right); page 53 (top left); page 57 (bottom right); page 64; page 75 (top); page 76 (bottom right); page 83 (bottom right); page 84 (top left; bottom right); page 87; page 90 (top left); page 91; page 94; page 97 (top left); page 99 (bottom left; bottom right); page 100 (top left; bottom left, bottom right); page 109 (top); page 116 (top left, bottom right); page 117 (bottom right; top left).

Additional information about herbs in mythology and throughout history from: Edinger, Philip (ed.), *How to Grow Herbs*, Menlo Park, California, Lane Books, 1972; Hamilton, Edith, *Mythology*, New York, New American Library, 1969; Loewenfeld, Claire and Philippa Back, *The Complete Book of Herbs and Spices*, New York, G.P. Putnam's Sons, 1974.

Table of Contents

1

Planning the Family Garden

Gardening can be a rewarding outdoor activity for the entire family. Careful planning will let you make the best use of the space you have and whatever time you and your family can devote to gardening.

The ideal garden, like the ideal home, begins on paper. Designing a family garden is, however, much easier than planning a house. While you begin in much the same way—measuring the area and considering orientation to the sun in relation to existing buildings, trees and shrubbery—you can always move or change a garden for a more effective use of existing space.

Preliminary Considerations

Planning a family garden requires more than simply deciding where to dig up a piece of the backyard to grow flowers and vegetables. You must first decide how much time you're willing to spend on your garden each day. A garden requires cultivating before planting, nurturing the plants as they grow, pulling weeds, eliminating or minimizing pests, and watering on a regular basis. If your time is limited, you'll want to limit your plans to something you can comfortably manage, even though your land will support a much larger garden.

Record keeping is a valuable tool for gardening success. Use a spiral-bound notebook to keep track of the varieties you plant. Use simple headings such as: Plant, Date Planted, Seed Type, Soil pH and Comments. If there is something else you would like to remember from season to season, be sure to include a heading for that information.

Raised beds are ideal for small gardens.

Row gardens require more space than other types but are the easiest to work.

Types of Gardens

There are four basic types of gardens: the conventional row or strip garden, the block-planted garden, the raised-bed garden and the container garden. You can have several types for specific plantings.

Conventional row or strip gardens are cultivated areas where you plant seeds or seedlings in rows. Success with a row garden depends, in part, on allowing enough space between the rows so you can weed, water and cultivate without damaging the plants. Row gardens require more space and are less productive than other types. Nevertheless, they are the most popular and the easiest to manage.

Block-planted gardens are commonly used for crops such as corn that require cross pollination.

This type also works well for peas, carrots, beets and lettuce. The overall size of the block planting should be about 20 square feet (4 ft. × 5 ft.) for smaller crops and as large as 20 feet square (20 ft. × 20 ft.) for crops such as corn. Cultivate the plot to a depth of about 8 inches. At the same time, work compost or peat moss and fertilizer into the soil. Next, broadcast the seeds lightly over the plot and, with the aid of a tiller or rake, work them into the soil to the proper depth. After the seedlings emerge, thin them to the recommended spacing. You can get high yields in this type of garden.

Raised-bed gardens are a good choice if you have limited space and poor soil conditions. You can build raised-bed frames from timbers, pressure-treated lum-

You can build raised-bed frames from redwood, cedar or pressure-treated lumber.

Row gardens are the most popular type.

Block gardens often require large areas.

ber or other suitable materials. Fill with good topsoil, compost and peat moss. Raised-bed gardens have some advantages. They generally drain well, the plants are easier to tend because they are raised above the ground, and you can plant vegetables closer together, giving a higher overall yield.

In container gardens plants grow in pots, window boxes and other containers. Urban residents, because they generally lack space, can plan to have entire gardens in containers. Country gardeners can also use them in their plans to bring parts of the garden— herbs, small tomatoes, even eggplants—closer to the house.

Containers must drain well, contain rich soil, and be large enough for proper root development. Some hybrid vegetables have been developed for container growing. The most difficult part is supplying adequate moisture to the growing plants, especially during the hot, dry summer months. The limited amount of soil in containers doesn't hold moisture very long.

Many vegetables have been developed specifically for container growing.

Container gardens can be anywhere.

Soil Preparation Planning

Planning for soil preparation and conditioning is important for gardening success.

You can't improve your soil until you determine what type you have and whether it is acid or alkaline. You'll need to make different plans to cultivate, fertilize and water if the type of soil you have is clay, sandy or loam.

Take soil samples to your local agricultural extension office for analysis. Do this well ahead of time. These offices may be backlogged in the early spring when everyone seems to want soil analysis, so you may not have the results back for three weeks. You can also buy an inexpensive soil testing kit and analyze the soil yourself.

Soil testing is simple with a kit available from seed companies or local nurseries.

After you know the kind and quality of your soil, you can make plans to improve it before planting. This will involve adding compost, peat moss or topsoil. You'll also have to add agricultural sulfur or ground limestone to adjust the acid-alkaline level of your soil.

Planning a Water Supply

Adequate water is an essential part of any successful garden. When planning you must consider how you'll get water to the growing plants. If your garden is close to the house, you can easily water with a hose and sprinkler. But, if your garden is more than 100 ft. away from a faucet, you'll spend too much time wrestling hoses and other watering equipment. A good solution is to install a ¾-in. polyvinyl chloride (PVC) plastic pipe from an existing water supply. The water line can be buried to conceal it or simply run overland. In cooler regions, install a drain valve so you can empty the entire system before a hard frost.

Planning Plantings

Once you decide on the overall layout of the plot, you will have to plan your crops annually. Every year, seed companies send out catalogs soon after the winter holidays. This is the time to begin making plans for your family garden. These annual catalogs will tell you what new varieties and seeds have been developed the previous season.

Decide what vegetables and flowers you'd like to grow. The list of possibilities is almost endless, but the amount of space you have is not. As you plan, hold your imagination in check. Your local climate may not be suitable for some plants. Let personal experience and information from your agricultural extension agent be your guide. You can't

Always have extra crops ready to be planted when space is available in the garden.

always trust that the general information about growing conditions in seed catalogs is correct for where you live. Try to limit the types of vegetables the first few years. Start with the easy crops such as tomatoes, broccoli, spinach, lettuce, radishes and summer squash and with flowers such as zinnias and marigolds.

Choose vegetables your family enjoys. Don't turn your garden into an agricultural experimental station. If no one in your family is fond of Swiss chard, don't waste time and space growing it.

The Approximate Space Chart in this chapter will help decide which vegetables to plant. Keep in mind that almost every year, seed companies introduce new "bush" type vegetables that take up much less space. For example, a standard cucumber plant requires about 5 sq. ft. of garden space but the new bush cucumbers need only about one-third the space—and may produce more cucumbers.

Succession Plantings

Gardening on a small plot will be most productive when you plan to have a succession of vegetables ready to plant as you harvest ripe crops. Plant peas in the early spring; then after the peas have been harvested, replant the area with tomato seedlings to ripen during the summer and early fall. Beans are another crop that mature early in the summer. After they have been harvested, use the space for broccoli, cauliflower, Brussels sprouts or turnips.

Whenever you plant a second crop during the summer months, you may face the possibility of losing it to an early frost. By choosing hardy vegetables such as spinach, chard, turnips, beets and any of the cabbage family, the plants should survive even if a light frost hits early. Vegetables that mature in the fall are generally better tasting and more suitable for long-term storage or canning.

To make sure you will always have extra plants on hand for transplanting, start seeds as early as 6 to 8 weeks before you put them out in the garden. In late winter and early spring you'll have the best success with a coldframe or small greenhouse for starting plants. A special grow table is another possibility when you don't have a coldframe or a greenhouse. After the last frost of the spring, however, you can raise the seedlings in containers. Then when space becomes available in the garden, you can transplant your new seedlings as you harvest other crops.

When seedlings are small, use any container but don't overcrowd the plants. As they grow, thin the plants to keep only the most hardy. After two sets of leaves develop, transplant the seedlings into larger pots where they will grow until put out in the garden. Some of the best seedlings to raise in nursery flats and other containers include: broccoli, lettuce, chard, Brussels sprouts, tomatoes, cucumbers, squash and most types of herbs.

If you're going to have flowers in your garden—and you should—these will require planning as well. You should try to have a continuing series of blooms throughout the season. While snow is still on the ground, crocuses can be sprouting, followed by daffodils, hyacinths and tulips. Soon after come the forsythia, azaleas and lilacs. Next, of course, are summer flowers. Grow a variety both for ornamentation and cutting. Flowers like daisies, marigolds and zinnias are good choices for summer flowers. If you have the space, try wildflower mixtures but pick the general type suitable for your area. There are wild flower mixtures for coastal, plains and mountain regions. You can cap off your season with the late summer and fall varieties of chrysanthemums and asters. Marigolds and zinnias will continue to bloom until the first frost.

Wildflower mixtures offer a variety of flowers that bloom all season long.

APPROXIMATE SPACE PLANTING CHART FOR VEGETABLES				
CROP	pH	SEED DEPTH (INCHES)	ROW SPACE (INCHES)	PLANT SPACING (INCHES)
Asparagus	6.0–7.0	6–8	36–48	12–18
Beans, lima	5.5–6.5	1–1½	24–36	3–4
Beans, snap	6.0–7.5	1–1½	24–36	1–2
Beets	6.0–7.0	¼–½	15–24	2–3
Broccoli	6.0–7.0	¼–½	24–36	12–18
Brussels sprouts	6.0–7.0	¼–½	24–36	18–24
Cabbage	6.0–7.0	¼–½	24–36	12–18
Cantalope	6.0–8.0	1	48–72	24–30
Carrots	5.5–6.5	¼–½	15–30	2–3
Cauliflower	6.0–7.0	¼–½	24–36	18–24
Celery	6.0–6.5	⅛	18–36	4–6
Chard, Swiss	6.0–7.0	¼–½	18–36	6–8
Collards	6.0–7.0	¼–½	24–36	18–24
Cucumber	6.0–8.0	1	48–60	12–18
Eggplant	6.0–7.0	¼	30–40	18–24
Endive	6.0–7.0	¼–½	18–36	12
Garlic	6.0–7.0	1½	18–24	3
Kale	6.0–8.0	¼–½	18–36	8–12
Kohlrabi	6.0–8.0	¼–½	18–36	4–6
Leeks	6.0–8.0	½	12–30	2–3
Lettuce	6.0–7.0	¼	12–18	6–10
Okra	6.0–8.0	1	36–48	12–18
Onions	6.0–7.0	1–2	15–24	3–4
Parsley	5.0–7.0	¼	15–24	6–8
Parsnips	6.0–8.0	½	18–30	3–4
Peas	6.0–8.0	1–2	8–24	1
Peppers	6.0–6.5	¼	30–42	18–24
Potatoes	4.8–6.5	4	30–36	12
Pumpkins	6.0–8.0	1	60–96	36–48
Radish	6.0–8.0	½	12–24	1
Rhubarb	6.0–8.0	4	36–48	36–48
Rutabaga	6.0–8.0	¼–½	18–30	3–4
Spinach	6.5–7.0	½	12–24	2–4
Spinach, N.Z.	6.0–7.0	½–1	30–42	15–18
Squash, Summer	6.0–8.0	1–1½	48–60	18–24
Squash, Winter	6.0–8.0	1–1½	60–96	36–48
Sweet corn	6.0–7.0	1–2	30–36	10–12
Sweet potatoes	6.0–7.0	4	30–36	12–15
Tomatoes	6.0–7.0	¼	36–60	24–36
Turnips	6.0–8.0	¼–½	18–30	2–3
Watermelon	6.0–7.0	1–1½	60–96	36–60

2

Children in Garden

Children love to be outdoors, and a family garden is a wonderful way for them to develop a sensitivity to living things and the natural forces that shape the world around us. In this era of instant foods, instant entertainment and instant energy, gardening is a way to introduce a basic understanding of life and to develop the patience to appreciate its process.

The family garden is a wonderful place for children to find things and learn about nature.

Between the time you plant a seed and harvest some food or enjoy some flowers, a whole cycle of activities and adventures emerges to challenge the young mind and imagination. Every day there are new changes as the seeds sprout, send up leaves, and the plant grows and develops.

A Place to Grow

Make your children feel welcome in the garden by giving them their own space. Pick an area that has some shade and make it a place where children can dig without restriction. Locate their garden area apart from the play area so they have a place for boisterous (and potentially destructive) play safely away from their garden activities. Raised-bed gardens are a treat for children because all the action takes place in a small space.

Include your children in your building projects, letting them help build the raised bed or redo the compost bins. In planting row gardens for your children, space the rows a little farther apart so their intense concentration on one plant does not result in total destruction of others.

A greenhouse is an ideal gardening environment for children. On cold days there will be a warm place to be, and gardening can be a year-round experience.

Growing Projects

It's important to allow children some latitude in the garden. If they want to move a plant to another spot, let them—even though this may not be something you would do. Let them decide what plants they will grow. These should, however, be skillfully guided decisions that will ensure them the greatest chance of success and learning excitement. Try to steer their decisions to crops that will almost always guarantee success. But be prepared to deal positively with the inevitable disappointment of failures. Know in advance that some time during the season a favorite plant is not going to make it and you're going to have to explain why. Work with your children to tell the difference between weeds and young plants of crops and flowers. Not all weeds have to be pulled, however. Growing a good crop of weeds may be just as exciting as growing radishes or daisies.

Let your children start with radishes or carrots. Ready for harvest a month after planting, results are fast. While radishes are quick to grow, fun to harvest and great to admire, your children may not care for their taste or texture. The rest of your family may have to eat more radishes than you planned on from your part of the garden.

Pole beans are a good growing project for children because the results can be dramatic. Beans planted to grow forming an Indian teepee or roof will continue to entertain your children all summer.

Even routine tasks are important to children as their contribution to the success of your family garden.

WATCHING PLANTS GROW

Here's a way to help your children understand what's happening to the seeds they've planted in the garden. Start with an empty peanut butter jar or large water glass. Pull about six paper towels off a roll and trim or fold them to the height of the jar. Roll the towel into a tube and slide it inside the jar. Place different kinds of beans between the towels and the glass side, then pour in water to keep the paper towels wet. Put the jar on a window sill or other warm, sunny place. The beans will soon grow roots and send a stem up over the top of the jar. When the second set of leaves develops on the bean plants and they are about 6 in. tall, you may want to put them in pots to plant in the garden later. Point out to your children that no matter which way the bean is "planted" in the jar, roots grow down and the stem grows up. What they see happening in the jar is exactly what's happening hidden in the soil of your family garden.

MYSTERY GARDEN

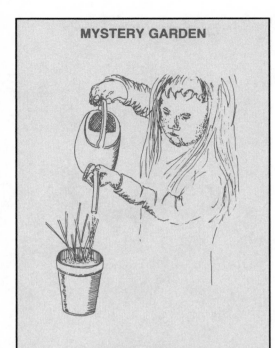

Here's a project for your children that will involve them in a little detective work and teach them more about the kinds of plants and weeds in their garden. Take your children to a park or a field near your home, preferably some weekend in the early spring. Dig down to where the soil is damp, and put a couple of handfuls of this soil in a paper cup. Poke holes in the bottom of the cup and water the soil until the water just starts to come through the holes. Put it in a sunny window at home. Whenever the top of the soil feels dry, your children can give it more water. Lots of seeds and dormant plants will be hiding in that soil. When the plants emerge and are established enough that you can identify them, dig out the garden books and help your children discover what kinds of plants they have growing in their mystery garden. Remember, even weeds need love, and children enjoy taking care of plants and watching them grow.

While the bean-pole structure is enjoyable, harvesting the ripe beans is even more fun. Since most pole beans bear over an extended period, picking can be a daily or every other day event. The popular Kentucky Wonder and Romano (Italian Pole) are two good choices.

Cucumbers are also fun to grow. Most children love the taste and texture of cucumbers, so *finding* the ripe vegetable is only half the fun. With a little help from you and the pickling jar, they can enjoy their cucumbers with sandwiches well beyond the gardening season. Good choices include Burpee Hybrid II, Early Pride Hybrid and Bush Champion. The latter is a bush-type variety that requires less garden space.

Another good crop for children to grow are pumpkins. The long vines snake through the garden and make finding the pumpkins an adventure. If garden space is limited, grow a bush-type variety such as Cinderella, which requires only 6 sq. ft. Harvest before the first frost, store in a cool place and you can have a party to carve jack-o-lanterns for Halloween.

The thrill of discovery in even the most simple of growing things is part of the joy of gardening for children.

Sweet corn is good for younger children to plant because the seeds are large and easy to handle. The plants emerge quickly and rise to almost unbelievable heights. Children love to report on the progress of their corn plants. When the tassels turn brown and harvest time comes, your children will want to help pick the corn. After picking, the fun continues with hot, buttered corn-on-the-cob on their plates.

As an alternative to sweet corn, encourage your children to plant Indian corn. Growth is just as dramatic but the chances of success are greater since even underdeveloped ears have color and variety in the kernels. The harvested crop of your children's Indian corn can decorate your tables and doors throughout the fall, and you can keep the dried ears for years.

Sunflowers grow big and tall, and children get a kick out of being responsible for something so large. After the sunflowers ripen, harvest and let them dry before storing. During the winter months, put a sunflower head outside the kitchen window so everyone can watch the birds come to feed.

Marigolds and zinnias are good flowers to include in the children's part of the garden. They'll bloom most of the summer, providing continued rewards for the effort put into planting them.

CARROT TOP GARDEN

In late winter when it's too early to work in the soil outside, but everyone is anxious for signs of spring, your children can get an early start on the gardening season with a carrot top garden. While there'll be no edible harvest, the lacy greens will be an attractive preview for the warmer months of spring when your family can get back out in the garden. Cut about an inch off the top of a carrot. Cut off any stems and leaves already on the carrot. Fill a shallow aluminum foil pie pan with a layer of coarse sand or gravel. Then put the cut carrot tops on top of the gravel and pour water into the dish. Put the dish in a bright spot but not in direct sun. Be sure the water covers about ¼ in. of the carrot top by adding water every couple of days. Children love to do this. In a week or two, new leaves will sprout and look like feathery ferns. Without expense or much trouble for you, your children will have grown new plants before they can garden outside.

Pumpkins are a good growing project for children and the results can often be dramatic.

A family garden would not be complete without strawberries. Combine some plants of the everbearing type with spring-bearing varieties so you can harvest them from spring throughout the summer. If space

LAWN ON A SPONGE

Your children might want to grow a lawn of their own—indoors. This is an easy project for them to do, and they will see results quickly. Have them put a sponge in a bowl or deep dish and fill the bowl about halfway with water. Sprinkle some grass seeds over the sponge. Gently push the seeds into the sponge with a fork or stick so they are dampened by the sponge, but not under water. Be sure the sponge stays wet by adding water to the dish every couple of days. Your children will have fun "watering their lawns." After a few weeks the grass will have grown enough for your children to begin "mowing." Let them trim the grass with a scissors, keeping it about an inch high. You can also use a sponge to grow parsley or chives from seeds. These herbs can be harvested directly from the sponge garden to give salads or soups a more personal touch for your children. Even when trimmed, the parsley or chives will keep on growing for continued harvest.

is limited, grow strawberries in a container, like a barrel with holes drilled in the sides. Good choices include Shortcake or Tristar for the garden, and Alpine for growing in containers.

Dangers in the Garden

Children must learn there are some inherent dangers in the family garden. Some plants can be eaten and some cannot. Some insects are friendly and some are not. Some tools are theirs, some are yours. To be a responsible parent, teach the differences early.

Natural Dangers. Young children, especially, may want to harvest and consume in one continuous motion. Teach them early the importance of thoroughly washing (perhaps even peeling some) crops before they are eaten. Even if you don't use chemical controls in the garden, some residual toxic substances may be in the soil or may have drifted over from your neighbors.

Prevent infection-prone scratches early by pointing out the sharp thorns on roses and some berry bushes.

Dangerous Plants. Poisonous plants children may come in contact with include rhubarb leaves, potato vines and the wild mushrooms that sprout during wet or damp periods. These are dangerous when eaten.

The flower garden can also contain poisonous plants. The most common include the bulbs of daffodils, hyacinths and narcissi. The seeds of the following flowers are poisonous: morning glory, sweet pea,

Gardening can be a family project with something for everyone to do.

castor bean and wisteria. Poisonous flowers include iris, lily-of-the-valley, foxglove, oleander, larkspur, periwinkle, bleeding heart and monkshood. All parts of azalea, mountain laurel and rhododendron **are toxic** to humans although you (and your children) may see larger animals like deer eating them safely.

There are many other dangerous plants and some may be common in your area. Find out what they are by contacting your agricultural extension service. Your local poison control center may have illustrated booklets with color photographs and descriptions of poisonous and dangerous plants.

Garden Pests. There are other dangers in the family garden besides poisonous plants. In certain parts of the country, ticks, biting insects and spiders may be present in large enough numbers to pose a health threat.

Children should also learn early that bees don't like to be bothered when they're out collecting nectar for the hive. A good first-aid treatment for bee and wasp stings is a paste made from meat tenderizer and water.

A good source of information about any dangerous insects in your area is your local agricultural extension agent.

In some parts of the country, poisonous snakes can pose a real danger to children—and to you—in the garden. Along the eastern coast of the United

Gardening joy for children continues up to and through harvest time as they share your prize crops.

SWEET POTATO VINE

A sweet potato vine is an ideal way for your children to develop a late-winter interest in gardening. Next time you're at the grocery store, buy a sweet potato that has little purple buds on it. Fill a quart jar with water and add a few pieces of charcoal—the kind sold for fish aquarium filters. This keeps the water sweet. Poke toothpicks partway in around the middle of the sweet potato. Find the flat scar on the potato where it was cut from the stem and put this end down in the water, with the toothpicks holding the rest of the potato above the top of the jar. Put the jar with the sweet potato in a shady spot until the roots begin to grow from the bottom and the vines begin to start from the top. This can take anywhere from a few days to a few weeks. You will have to add more lukewarm water every couple of days. When the vines and roots begin to appear, move the potato to a bright sunny spot. Your children can help grow the vine around a window making a living window frame.

States, copperheads and water moccasins may slither into your garden. Rattlesnakes can be common in the high plains and mountainous regions. Many times you'll have temporary infestations of snakes in new housing developments where construction has disturbed their underground homes. Teach your children to be alert for snakes, especially in the early evening as outside temperatures begin to cool and these cold-blooded creatures move out to warm themselves on the cultivated soil of your garden.

Dangerous Tools. Regard all garden tools as a source of danger when children are around. Keep tools in one storage place until you need them. Youngsters love to work with tools in the garden. You can, and should, encourage this with tools designed especially for young children. As they mature in their gardening attitudes and develop more coordinated hand skills, let them use your "real" tools.

Importance of Supervision. You can eliminate or minimize many dangers with supervision by parents or responsible older children. For children under five years of age, supervision is important to establish a basic understanding and respect for growing plants. If you start early to educate your children about plants, later problems will be minimized and gardening will be fun for them.

Your guidance and help will make gardening a valuable learning experience for your children.

HEALTHY SPROUTS A FUN PROJECT

Buy some alfalfa seeds at a health food store. All you need is one ounce. This is enough for about five quart jars full of sprouts. Have your children soak about two tablespoons of seeds in a small cup or jar overnight. A quart mayonnaise jar is good. Help the children punch some holes in the top of the jar lid— or stretch a piece of cheesecloth or waxed paper with holes and secure it to the top of the jar with a rubber band. Put the jar on its side on a warm window sill or other spot where there is indirect sun. Have the children rinse the seeds in a colander or strainer with water twice a day and drain well each time. Put them back in the jar, loosen with a fork if they stick together, and cover the jar again. Children love to see the sprouts grow—and they will be ready to eat in just four or five days. Put the sprouts in direct sun for a few hours, cool them in the refrigerator, and your children can garnish their own sandwiches.

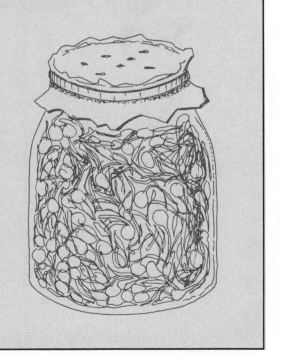

Family Gardening

Make gardening a family project with tasks for every family member. Don't forget that even the youngest child is an important part of the family circle in gardening. While you do the cultivating and other strenuous or potentially dangerous jobs, your children can help you with the weeding, harvesting and watering. Make a game out of finding fruits and vegetables ready for harvest. In a short time you'll be amazed at how much your children have learned about gardening, and perhaps you'll notice they have a new respect for living things. Make it a pleasant experience and you'll have years of joy to share with your children in the garden.

Patience is one of the qualities of life children learn when they're included with the family in gardening.

TRASH BAG POTATO FARM

Children can learn about the mystery of growing edible plants underground with their own inside "potato farm." Have them put about 3 or 4 quarts of soil into a small plastic trash bag and fold the top of the bag down. Select potatoes that have already begun to sprout and cut them into pieces making sure each piece has at least two sprouts. Plant about three of these 5 in. deep in the soil. Water the soil lightly every few days. When each plant grows to about 5 in. tall, select the healthiest plant to save and cut off the others. Keep the trash bag in a sunny spot, leaving it open and watered enough so it is moist but never soggy. Teach your children patience! They will see the gradual growth of the leaves while the dramatic, important growth of the potato is hidden under the soil. In about five or six weeks, let them feel underneath each plant to find the little potatoes. Check the size of the potatoes gently every couple of days and let your children decide when they would like to harvest their own crop and enjoy the fruits of home-grown potatoes.

3

Gardening Tools

Home gardening is fun, and the rewards are edible. There is also some work involved from the time you decide to grow flowers or vegetables until harvest time. This chapter introduces you to some of the hand tools, power tools, watering devices and sprayers that will make this work easier.

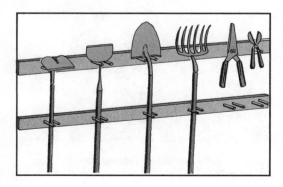

HAND TOOLS

A variety of hand tools is necessary for any size garden. Your collection of hand tools is probably the largest investment you'll make for your garden. But with a little care, tools will last for many years. The basic hand tools you'll need include shovels, rakes, forks, cultivators, and pruning tools.

Shovels and Trowels

While it's entirely possible to garden with only one shovel, there are special designs for specific tasks.

A long-handled spade with a rounded point is useful for digging, mixing and moving soil—a task made much easier with a long handle than with a short shovel.

A shovel with a short handle and rounded point is used for close-quarter digging, mixing, digging trenches and turning soil.

A shovel with a long handle and long narrow blade will be necessary if you're digging fence post holes or planting trees.

Trowels are small, one-handed shovels you use to plant seedlings, bulbs and annuals. When buying a hand trowel, look for solid construction and a tool that fits your hand well. Inexpensive hand trowels bend or break when working in hard soil.

Any shovel will last for years if you take care of it properly. Store shovels out of the weather when you're not using them. Hose or brush off dirty shovels before storing. Keeping the tools clean and sharp will extend their lives. A light coat of oil will help

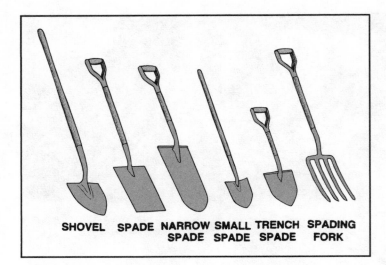

SHOVEL SPADE NARROW SMALL TRENCH SPADING
                SPADE   SPADE SPADE   FORK

Choose the right type of shovel for the digging task at hand.

prevent rust. You can apply a spray lubricant or work the shovel up and down in a pail of oiled sand.

A sharp shovel works best. To sharpen, use a flat file to work the cutting edge, following the original angle of bevel. Don't get the cutting edge too thin or it will nick or chip.

Rakes, Forks, Cultivators and Hoes

Rakes are handy when you want to cultivate soil, consolidate garden debris, smooth seed beds or renew your lawn.

Bow rakes have stiff metal or heavy plastic tines about 2 in. long. You can use these rakes to break

A hand trowel is the right tool for transplanting small seedlings.

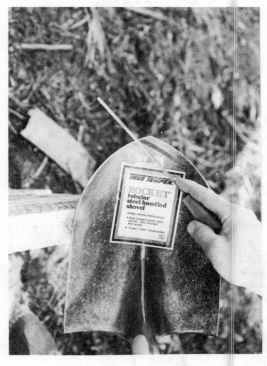

Use a round file to sharpen a shovel blade and digging will be easier.

up soil into a fine texture after cultivating. They are also useful for removing large debris from the garden or taking out the thatch from the base of the grass on your lawn.

Leaf rakes are available in metal, bamboo and plastic. The metal versions last for years. Bamboo leaf rakes are lightweight, inexpensive and effective but may last only one season. Plastic leaf rakes are now very popular and combine the long-lasting advantages of metal rakes with the lightweight flexibility of bamboo.

Pitch forks are used for turning compost and light cleanup in the garden. Most are not designed for any type of digging because the tines can bend or break.

Spading forks are used for turning soil and digging potatoes and other root crops. They penetrate deeper than shovels and break up the soil as it is turned over.

Cultivating tools come in several different types, but the most familiar is the three-tined cultivator. Use this tool to break up the surface of the soil around plants and to remove weeds. You'll find the long-handled type useful for general cultivating while you'll use the shorter hand cultivator for working around tight groupings of plants.

A spading fork is the right tool to use for first breaking up soil.

Rake a seedbed before planting and use the bow rake to form raised rows.

A pitch fork is the best tool for turning compost. Turn small amounts to avoid back injury.

The scuffle hoe works on both the forward and backward stroke.

Garden hoes have many uses. You can use them for light cultivation around plants, weed removal, breaking up crusted soil and for digging furrows. Keep a sharp cutting edge on your hoe and you can do your tasks with little effort.

The scuffle hoe is a new type of cultivator. It looks like a hoe but can be both pushed and pulled during use. You'll find this tool handy for removing weeds just below the soil line. You can use the scuffle hoe while standing and with a small amount of effort so there is little pressure on your lower back.

Pruning Tools

There is a variety of tools available to help you make good pruning cuts in the garden and orchard. You'll need both a one-handed model for light pruning and a two-handed tool for cutting branches as big as 2 in. across.

Single-handed pruning shears are for light pruning. They are available in two basic types: anvil and bypass, describing the blade configuration. Anvil type shears can't trim as closely as the bypass type. You may need both types for your different pruning tasks.

The anvil style has a single blade that cuts against a brass or plastic anvil which is simply a flat surface, softer than the blade. Place the branch being cut between the blade and the anvil so the blade passes through the branch and comes to rest on the anvil.

Bypass shears have a blade and a hook. As you press the handles together, the blade passes by the hook and cuts the branch. The bypass shear design will let you trim off a branch close to the main runner of the bush or trunk of the tree.

There are also single-handed draw-cut type shears. These operate much the same as a pair of scissors. You use these mainly for trimming grass, but they can also be used for light pruning jobs on your plants.

Three hand pruners (l. to r.): All purpose draw-cut snip, bypass pruner and anvil pruner.

Use long-handled loppers to cut material up to about 2 in. diameter.

Lopping shears are much the same as single-handed pruners except that they are used with both hands for pruning branches up to 2 in. diameter. Lopping shears are available in both anvil and bypass blade designs. Because of the long handles, they are better when you need to reach into thorned berry patches or rows of bushes to cut the canes. Long handles offer much greater leverage for cutting thick branches.

Pruning saws are invaluable for branches larger than about 1 in. diameter. Never try to force pruning shears through a branch. If shears won't make the cut easily, use a saw. Pruning saws also make quick cuts in green, wet wood. The teeth cut on both the forward and backward stroke. The teeth are large and widely spaced so the saw does not bind up or clog with wet sawdust. There are several different types of pruning saws from one-handed models to pole saws used for cutting high branches.

Because pruning tools will see many hours of use, you should sharpen them before the season. Sharpening is a good wintertime project. You must remove any nicks on the cutting blade and restore the original bevel. You can do this easily by using a flat file or small pocket sharpening stone. If the cutting blade is severely damaged, take your pruning tool to a professional sharpening service. After sharpening, oil the spring and blades.

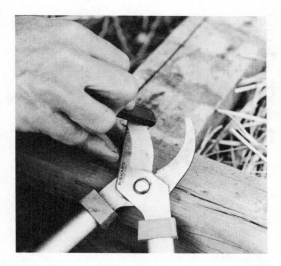

Sharpen the cutting blade on loppers or pruners with a small pocket stone.

Long-handled pruning saws reach high into trees and are good for large jobs.

Wheelbarrows and Carts

You'll find a good wheelbarrow indispensable. The best will have a pneumatic tire for easy pushing over all types of ground. A good wheelbarrow is balanced and easy to push when loaded. Some have a plastic tub which will not rust.

Large-wheeled garden carts are even more useful than the standard wheelbarrow. While these may be more expensive, they have a greater carrying capacity and require very little effort to move around.

POWER TOOLS

As garden space increases so does the need for more efficient tools to help make your work easier. You have a wide choice of machines and powered tools that will take much of the effort out of working the soil in your garden.

Tillers

Without a doubt, the hardest task in your garden is cultivating the soil. To prepare planting rows and seed beds properly, you'll turn over and break up tons of soil. You'll also have to mix in organic material such as compost and peat moss to improve the overall condition of the soil. While you can do this with a shovel and spading fork if your garden is small, a tiller will save hours of work and do a better job on larger gardens.

There are many different brands and styles of tillers available, but they all fall into one of two basic categories: front tine and rear tine tillers. Tines are the blades that dig up the soil as they rotate on the tiller.

A good wheelbarrow is indispensable for a variety of back-breaking tasks.

Small tillers are ideal for small gardens, and work well in raised beds.

Front tine tillers can handle all home gardening tasks. They are less expensive than rear tine tillers and you'll find a larger selection to choose from. A shortcoming of front tine tillers, however, is that the machine passes over the area you've just worked and the weight tends to compact the tilled soil.

The newly introduced mini front tine tillers are ideal for a variety of cultivating operations. These small units are lightweight (20 lbs.) and extremely efficient at tilling a swath 9 in. wide and 6 to 8 in. deep. You'll find these useful for tilling raised-bed gardens, row gardens and flower beds. Small tillers can be pushed *or* pulled which helps prevent compacting the soil.

Rear tine tillers are generally more heavy duty than front tine tillers. For large gardens rear tine tillers will do your job more quickly and with less effort. Rear tine tillers are more expensive, but if you have a large garden, these heavy duty machines may be a worthwhile investment.

There are other features you should consider when you shop for a garden tiller. After you've decided on either a front or rear tine, you should look for easy maintenance in a tiller. Since all are gasoline powered, look to see if the models you're considering are two or four cycle. Remember, you'll have to mix oil with gasoline for a two cycle engine.

If you're considering a large tiller, look for one that's self-propelled for both forward and reverse. Wheel weights or front weight kits—a common accessory on larger tillers—help balance the tiller and make it easier to use.

You can use some of the larger self-propelled tillers for other chores around your home. A plow blade, for example, will let you scrape and grade pathways and driveways. It's also ideal for pushing snow. The tines on these tillers disengage or are easily removed.

Heavy-duty rear tine tillers are best for large gardening projects.

Large gardens and lawn areas are easy to work with a tractor.

Garden Tractors

If your plans call for hard cultivating and hauling, you might want to consider a garden tractor. While these small tractors can't do everything a farm tractor can do, they are versatile. Some will let you attach a large mower, cutting a swath up to 50 in. wide. Cultivating and plowing are done with other attachments. Some models will even power a front loader or log splitter. While most garden tractors have gasoline engines, some of the newest and largest types are diesel powered.

This large chipper/shredder makes short work of cleaning up debris.

Chipper/Shredders

While not an essential gardening tool, a chipper/shredder can be a real aid around almost any garden.

You'll find a wide range of chipper/shredders from small electric units to tractor-mounted (power takeoff operated) professional machines. Prices begin at around $100 for the small electric powered shredders and climb to almost ten times that for the large machines. The more expensive chipper/shredders will generally do more than the lower priced units.

The new electric shredders are becoming popular with gardeners. Most are imported from Europe, and the overall quality and safety features are high. They'll chip branches up to 2 in. diameter but are made for chipping and shredding lighter materials such as corn stalks and other green garden refuse.

You'll find a chipper/shredder ideal for cleaning up around the garden. Since even a small garden will generate hundreds of pounds of organic waste, it makes good sense to recycle this material as com-

With a chipper/shredder it's easy to convert corn stalks into mulch.

post. Part of the secret of making good compost quickly is to shred all organic waste material before adding it to the compost pile. While you can simply pile garden waste to decompose naturally, you can speed up the process dramatically by shredding the material first. For example, it may take a year or more for broccoli plants to totally decompose. When the spent plants have been shredded first, compost matures in just a few months. The overall quality of this compost will be much better for your soil.

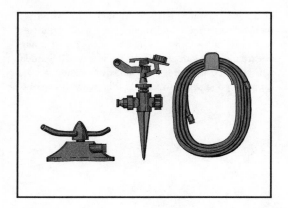

WATERING DEVICES

There is a variety of watering devices available—from automatic sprinkling systems to hose attachments. If a system or attachment can help you water your garden or lawn efficiently and easily, then it is probably a worthwhile investment.

Sprinklers

There are four types of sprinklers available: rotary, oscillating, impact and misting.

Rotary sprinklers are probably the least expensive. They are reasonably effective at spraying water through two or three arms rotating around the base. Major disadvantages are that they spread water in a circle and apply water at a rate most soils cannot absorb. Puddles and runoff can become a problem.

Oscillating sprinklers spread water in an even pattern. They are a good choice for conventionally shaped gardens. Less expensive units take more time than necessary at the end of each stroke and puddling can be a problem. On windy or especially dry days, oscillating sprinklers will cause more water to evaporate than soak into the soil.

A rotary sprinkler is inexpensive but may apply water too fast to absorb.

Impact sprinklers are widely used by farmers, ranchers and commercial growers. You can benefit from these efficient sprinklers on a much smaller scale by using a single impact sprinkler. The spray pattern is circular and you can adjust the streams of water—usually with some type of pin arrangement—to give off a long-range shot of water or a mist spray.

Misting sprinklers force water through tiny holes that produce a very fine spray. While this type of sprinkler will not cover a large area—no more than 20 ft. diameter—it does apply water in a fine mist easily accepted and absorbed by most garden soils.

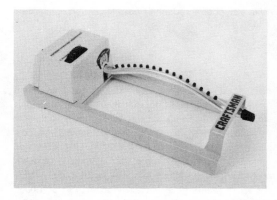

Oscillating sprinklers spread water in an even pattern over a wide area.

An impact sprinkler can give you the advantage enjoyed by farmers.

Drip irrigation systems are effective in the family garden.

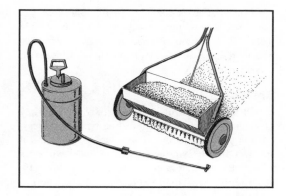

SPRAYERS AND SPREADERS

There is a variety of products available to make applying fertilizers and insecticides easier and safer in your garden.

Irrigation Systems

Drip irrigation systems are much more efficient than any other watering means because they deliver water only where it is needed. Plant stress is less with this type of watering, and the root systems develop quickly.

Most drip systems have a length of porous hose or have evenly spaced holes all along a hose. Other systems may have a main water line with tiny drip irrigators to water specific plants or areas.

Drip irrigation systems offer several advantages over conventional watering methods. Because most have some type of flow restrictor, they use less water over a given period. A typical system will have a flow rate of about 9 gallons of water an hour and a pressure of about 1 lb. per square inch.

Sprayers

You probably will need a sprayer to apply fertilizer and sometimes insecticides during the growing season. The simplest type attaches to the end of a hose and uses water pressure to apply the material. You can also use this to apply fertilizers and insecticides to your lawn.

There are also sprayers that use compressed air from a hand pump to apply material. These units are portable and effective for most spraying needs.

Electric-powered sprayers have a large capacity tank—from 12 to 25 gallons. These wheeled units are useful for large gardens and orchards. A typical model will have a rechargeable 12-volt battery system and a regulator to maintain even pressure inside the holding tank.

Small, pump-up sprayers are handy for small garden spraying jobs.

Power sprayer mounted on cart can handle any spraying task, large or small.

Clean your garden sprayer thoroughly after use. Some solutions contain compounds which corrode metal. Use kerosene followed by a soapy water solution to remove all traces of the spray. Rinse with water and dry before storing.

Spreaders

You'll find a fertilizer spreader handy for a variety of gardening tasks. There are two types: broadcast or rotary; and the drop spreader. A mechanical spreader will let you cover garden and lawn areas with fertilizer, limestone or sulfur more efficiently and evenly than simply spreading these materials by hand.

The least expensive of all spreaders are those hand held units that broadcast seed or fertilizer with the turn of a crank handle. Fertilizer or other material is loaded into the top and, as the handle is turned, drops onto a rotating wheel which broadcasts the material out the front at the bottom in a semicircle pattern. During use it's important to keep moving forward and watch to see that material is not being applied too heavily in one spot. Most units have an adjustment screw to increase or decrease the amount of material being dispensed.

Drop spreaders are handy for applying any granular material to large garden areas before you begin cultivating. Drop spreaders are adjustable, and flow is usually regulated by a sliding gate that controls the size of the openings at the base of the speader. Materials of different consistencies drop at different rates, so be sure to read the directions on any material for drop-spreader settings.

A small rotary spreader will broadcast material in a semicircular pattern.

4

Building Projects

A wide assortment of garden structures and aids is available for your family garden. If you're handy with a hammer and saw, you can easily build many of these yourself. You'll not only save hundreds of dollars, you will also gain the satisfaction of adding your own personal craft touch to your family garden.

Lumber for Outdoor Use

You must use either pressure-treated lumber or heart redwood in any building project where the wood will come in contact with the soil.

With the exception of heart redwood, all untreated dimensional lumber (2×4, 2×6, 2×8, 2×10, for example) is subject to damage by wood-eating insects such as termites and to rot and decay by fungus. Fungus is a living plant and certain strains can and do attack wood. As a fungus feeds on wood fibers, the wood decays and loses much of its strength. You'll find fungus spores in the soil, but they can also be airborne.

Untreated wood, especially in contact with the soil or exposed to weather, has an effective life of three to five years. Pressure-treated lumber has been tested to last many more years with no deterioration when used either above or below the ground.

Wood properly treated with chromated copper arsenate (CCA-treated) generally needs no protective coating, even for "frequent human contact" uses such as decks, planting boxes or picnic tables. CCA-treated lumber is safe to use indoors when sawdust and construction debris are cleaned up and disposed of after construction.

Lumber has been pressure-treated since Biblical times. Some of the methods result in a potentially toxic product and these, obviously, should be avoided. A good example of toxic treatment is the creosote used in preserving railroad ties. Use of wood products that have a toxic residue may have short- or long-term ill effects on your garden, your health and the general health of anyone who comes in contact with it. If you're going to use pressure-treated lumber, buy only lumber that has a label telling you it was treated according to approved guidelines.

Two basic types of preservatives are in general use—one is oil-based the other waterborne. The wood is submerged and pressure is applied forcing chemicals into the pores. The green color seen in some treated woods is the result of waterborne salts, such as inorganic arsenicals. Oil-based preservatives generally give wood a dark brown, almost black color.

When working with any treated lumber, be sure to observe some basic safety rules. Wear eye protection, a dust mask and gloves. Avoid inhaling sawdust

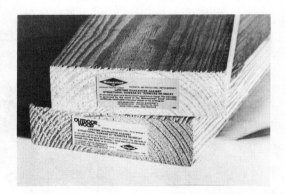

Properly treated dimensional lumber will have a label that shows compliance with EPA standards.

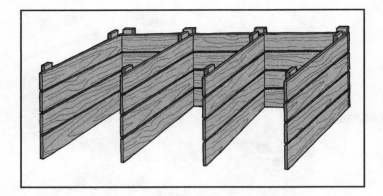

To build this **wooden compost bin** you'll need sixteen pieces of 2×12 lumber cut into 3 ft. lengths. You'll also need four 2×12s, 12 ft. long for the back. Six 2×4s 4 ft. long will serve as posts. Attach the sides as shown, letting each 2×4 extend about 12 in. below the side and back. You'll put these in post holes. Then attach the side to the rear with nails or lag bolts. Use redwood, cedar or pressure-treated lumber.

from this wood. Wash thoroughly with soap and water after handling treated wood. Seal the wood when you use it for frequently used areas such as benches or decks.

Redwood, while more expensive, is a good alternative for outdoor building projects. Redwood has no toxicity, it is easy to work with, and your finished projects will look beautiful. Heart redwood has a natural resistance to weather and diseases that attack other woods. Some grades of redwood that you'll find in lumber yards, however, are not all heartwood but have some cream-colored sapwood. Sapwood is **not** decay resistant and should be used only above the ground.

Apply a linseed oil-based sealer to redwood to minimize checking, cupping or splintering. These are natural aging signs that will appear on all lumber used outdoors, treated or not.

Use hot-dipped galvanized nails for all outdoor projects. Common steel nails rust, leaving an ugly stain.

Composters

It makes sense to compost the bushels of organic refuse your garden will give up in a season. While it's possible to make compost by simply piling organic

waste material on the ground, composting is easier with some type of bin arrangement. Composting bins help contain the matter and keep the garden tidy. But their main purpose is to contain the heat generated by decaying matter and encourage the growth of bacteria to aid in the process.

The drawings in this chapter show general types of composting units. These types differ in the material used for construction, but the overall principle of building a unit with three compartments is the common element.

Raised Beds for Gardens

Many feel the time, effort and money spent on building a raised bed for a garden is well worth it. Once it is properly built of treated lumber or redwood, a raised bed should provide decades of usefulness. Raised beds are easier to cultivate. While they are handy for your whole garden if you have limited space, raised beds are also a worthwhile project for small herb gardens, berry patches and flower gardens.

Raised garden beds can be simple or complex. If you follow some basic construction guidelines, the structure will not bulge or fall apart from the weight of the soil inside. You can build a simple raised bed from 1×4 or 1×6 lumber stood on edge and

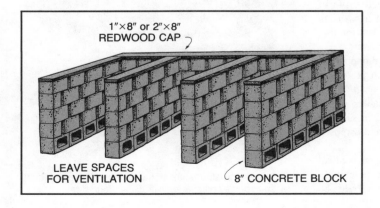

Compost bin made of **concrete blocks**.

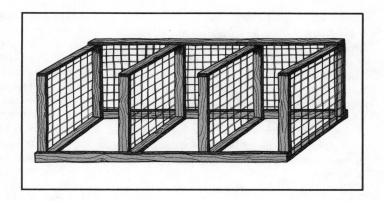

To build the **wire mesh compost bin** you'll need three 10 ft. lengths and four 12 ft. lengths of 2×4, and twenty-one pieces of 2 in. wire mesh cut into 3×4 ft. pieces. Select heart redwood, · cedar or pressure treated lumber for all parts. Use the 12 ft. long lumber to build the 3 ft. side frames. You'll need four sides. Attach a 3×4 ft. section of wire mesh to each side frame. Then attach the side frames to 10-ft.-long 2×4s that form the top, back and front. Use lag bolts.

filled with good soil. You can make a more attractive and useful raised-bed garden from 2×6 or 2×8 lumber, two or more boards high. A 2×6 top plate will add rigidity to the sides and give you a seat for working.

No matter which basic design you use, stake the unit in place to prevent bulging. The best approach is to construct the raised bed in place first, then drive 2×4 stakes around the perimeter spaced at 2-ft. intervals. Then fasten the raised bed to the stakes. You can also put these stakes inside the raised bed if you want a neater overall appearance. Stakes should extend far enough into the ground to provide solid support and should be trimmed off at the rim of the raised bed.

Before you fill the bed with topsoil and compost, cultivate the bottom as deeply as possible. If the soil is mainly clay, add sand to help drainage. In extreme cases you may have to add a layer of gravel to the bottom before filling.

Raised-bed gardens are a worthwhile building project, especially if you have limited space.

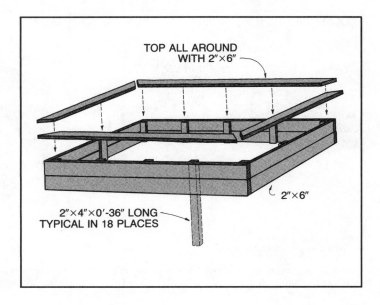

TOP ALL AROUND WITH 2″×6″

2″×6″

2″×4″×0′-36″ LONG TYPICAL IN 18 PLACES

Building a frame for a raised bed can be a quick weekend afternoon project

Coldframes and Hotbeds

A coldframe can be as simple as an old window covering a wooden box or as complex as a battery of internally heated growing chambers. Any coldframe can pay for itself the first season. Just in starting many of the vegetables you'll be growing, seeds are always less expensive than seedlings from a nursery. You can also start annual flowers in a coldframe and they'll be hardier than annuals started indoors.

Coldframes can either be free standing or built against the south wall of an existing building. Dimensions will vary but a unit measuring 4 ft. wide by 4 ft. long is a suitable size for most small gardens.

A coldframe lets you get a jump on the gardening season by starting seeds or annual flowers.

The back should be at least twice as high as the front to help shed rainwater and snow. Build the frame from dimensional lumber—1×12 for the back and 1×6 for the front with diagonally cut 1×12s for the sides. You can also use ½-in. or ¾-in. exterior plywood for the basic box. If you use plywood, reinforce the corners with 2×2 lumber.

For glazing you can use old storm windows or storm doors (common items at garage sales), sheet acrylic or corrugated fiberglass panels. A frame for the glazing should fit snugly over the coldframe box. Use a piano hinge along the back edge for easier opening and closing. You can use this basic design to start a variety of plants.

To make the coldframe more useful, consider installing a heat cable to the bottom of the unit. A heated coldframe is commonly called a **hotbed**. Heat cable (the kind used to prevent plumbing from freezing) with a thermostat is also useful to keep a constant soil temperature inside a coldframe. An inside temperature of 68°F is ideal during the pre-gardening season.

To make a hotbed, begin by digging out about 1 ft. of dirt from inside the coldframe. Add about 8 in. of pea gravel for drainage. Next lay out the cable in an "S" pattern over the gravel and cover with builders sand. If you're planting seeds directly in the hotbed rather than in seed flats, it's a good idea to lay a piece of hardware cloth over the heat cable before putting in the sand. Then add the growing medium: sand, compost and topsoil.

Both coldframes and hotbeds are ideal for growing small plants. Keep an eye on the weather. If it's

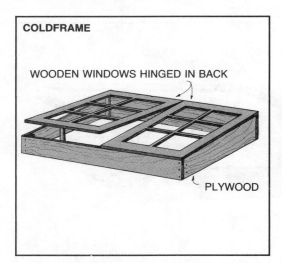

Build your coldframe to the dimensions that suit your needs and space best.

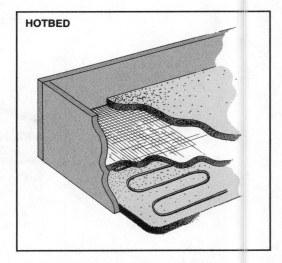

This hotbed will do some gardening on its own by automatically controlling temperature level.

cold, keep the cover closed. If it turns warm, open the cover to let excess heat escape. Close the unit in the late afternoon to capture heat for the night. In colder climates, mound soil, hay, leaves or other material around the outside of the coldframe as added insulation. If extreme weather is predicted, cover the entire coldframe with a tarp. Remove as soon as the weather breaks.

For a handy heat source, especially in early spring, use 2-liter soft drink bottles, painted black and filled with water. When set along the back edge of the coldframe, they will absorb heat during direct sunlight and give off heat through most of the night. This will produce a moderating effect and, as a result, plants will generally do better than if grown without these make-shift heaters.

Cloches

A cloche is a tent-like tunnel placed as a protective cover over a garden row or raised bed to get an early start or to extend the growing season. Cloches have been used for many years in Europe and are becoming increasingly popular with gardeners on this continent. Commercially made units are available, but most gardeners make their own cloches.

Probably the most common materials for home-made cloches are polyvinyl chloride (PVC) plastic pipe and clear polyethylene plastic. Other choices for the frame include 9-gauge wire, concrete reinforcing wire mesh and standard lumber. You can also use saplings to make the frame.

The basic design of a cloche is a tunnel. This shape stands up well to winds, while rain and snow

fall off quickly. The area you want to cover will dictate the width, and length. For example, if you're covering a row of lettuce, make a cloche tunnel about 4 in. wider on each side than the row. Determine the height by the plants themselves. The ends of your cloche must be movable so the tunnel can be ventilated during warm weather and closed at night and during cold weather. While a cloche will warm the soil inside, it will not hold heat. If cold is predicted, cover the cloche with a tarp at night. Two-liter plastic bottles, painted black and filled with water, will help moderate interior temperatures.

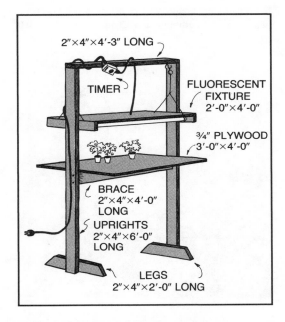

Grow table you can build in your workshop.

This cloche in a commercial nursery is almost as large as a greenhouse.

A cloche is a good way to get an early start on the gardening season.

Grow Tables

Many gardeners start seeds indoors eight weeks before the last expected frost. To be successful this early, you need to supply the tiny seedlings with adequate light. This may only be possible with special grow lights available from gardening centers. Suspend the fluorescent fixture (a 4-tube unit is better than a 2-tube unit) with rope and put a pulley on each side. Fasten the rope to cleats on the uprights. Adjust the height of the fixture one side at a time. Install an automatic timer, such as those sold for turning house lights on and off, to ensure a 14-hour minimum of light per day.

Greenhouses

Every gardener dreams of a greenhouse to raise exotic plants, start seedlings and grow vegetables year round.

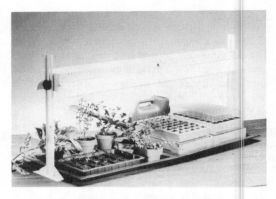

Grow table is a good way to start seedlings weeks before you can in the garden.

When you consider buying a greenhouse, think about the basic type and size you want. Consider also the type of glazing—you can get glass or plastic. Then consider if you want the greenhouse to be freestanding or attached to your house. Another obvious consideration is, of course, how much you can afford to spend.

You need to consider how you will vent the greenhouse. This is important during the hot summer days. Consider too how the greenhouse will be heated during cold days and nights.

You can also build your own greenhouse. Since many manufacturers sell glazing material and other important greenhouse components, you could easily build a custom greenhouse for less than a prefabricated unit.

The ideal greenhouse, one that takes care of itself, must be able to store heat so the interior temperatures remain moderate. There are several ways you can do this, including building the greenhouse partly underground. Since the temperature of the earth below

Freestanding greenhouse can be put almost anywhere.

Attached greenhouse adds a sunspace to your house.

Automatic venting controls will open glazing when interior temperatures of greenhouse rise too high.

the surface soil is fairly constant, a greenhouse in a partial excavation will have a more moderate internal temperature than a greenhouse on top of the ground. This holds true regardless of the climate in your area.

Another way to moderate the temperature is to use mass. "Mass" simply means using heat storage materials in the structure that are slow to heat or cool. Good choices include concrete, masonry, rock and jugs of water.

There are also commercial, but expensive, materials designed to capture and radiate solar energy. These include phase-change materials such as calcium chloride hexahydrate and special salts.

Greenhouses are much easier to use when you have easy access to water. While a small unit may use only 5 to 10 gallons of water daily, larger units will require much more.

Venting systems are a necessity during warmer weather. Internal temperatures can easily reach 100°F on a spring day. You can make vents in the gable ends or install movable ceiling glazing. In hot weather, use fans to move the excess heat out and prevent mildew or mold. Automatic venting systems with temperature sensors are best.

Mesh Fencing Material Projects

Wire fencing is a handy material to have around your garden. Use chicken wire, in 2-ft.-high sections, to make pea trellises. Drive 2-in.-sq. × 4-ft.-long posts into the ground at 4- to 6-ft. intervals and attach the wire. Plant seeds on both sides of the wire (a north-south orientation is ideal) and the peas will grow up the wire for easy picking. Choose pea varieties that grow to a 2-ft. height, such as Sugar Ann.

Concrete reinforcing wire with a 4×6-in. mesh is good for tomato cages. Smaller mesh is also suitable but the holes will have to be cut and enlarged to pick the ripe tomatoes.

Concrete reinforcing wire can be used to make cages to support your tomato plants.

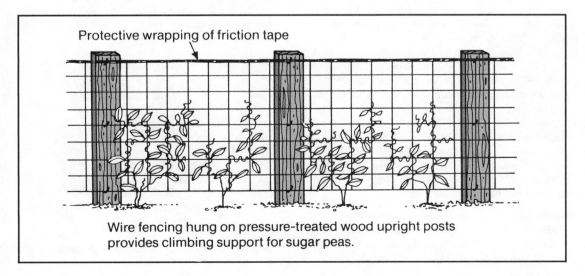

Protective wrapping of friction tape

Wire fencing hung on pressure-treated wood upright posts provides climbing support for sugar peas.

Sifting screens are easy to construct and have a variety of uses in the garden.

Gardening Aids

You can build other gardening aids in your home workshop—including a variety of sifting screens, seedling flats, planters and garden benches.

Sifting Screens. Screens are handy for sifting compost, sifting fine soil for seeds and for removing rock and debris from the soil where you'd like to grow root crops. All sifting screens are made the same way, but the size and mesh of screening will differ depending on how you intend to use it. For example, a small screen for sifting potting soil should measure about 12×18 inches. Construct the frame from 1×2 lumber and cover with small mesh hardware cloth. A larger screen with wider spaced mesh is useful for sifting soil by the shovelful. Use the largest size—4 ft.×4 ft.—to sift compost. Poultry netting with a mesh of ½ in. to 1 in. diameter is good material for this large screen.

Build small screens from 1×2 lumber and larger screens with 2×4 lumber. Attach screening with a stapler, tacks or roofing nails.

Seed Flats. Seed flats are indispensable for starting seedlings. They can also hold peat pots and carry seedlings to the garden. You're sure to find use for several of these handy trays throughout the season.

The most durable seed flats are made from 1×4 lumber for the side frame with cedar strips, perforated hardboard or ¼-in.-thick plywood for the bottom. If you use perforated hardboard, it must be a waterproof type or it will deteriorate. The bottom of the seed flat can be nailed to the bottom of the frame, or you can cut a groove on the inside of the frame to accommodate the bottom.

Benches. Benches give you a place to relax between gardening chores and provide a handsome place to put potted plants. The plans shown in this chapter suggest using redwood, a long-lasting, beautiful natural wood.

Do-it-Yourself Help

The Popular Mechanics *Do-it-Yourself Encyclopedia* contains a wealth of detailed information and construction plans for other projects you can build for your garden.

You'll get more detailed information about using pressure-treated lumber or redwood in your building projects in various sections of the *Encyclopedia*. General explanations of treated lumber and grades of redwood are in the article, "What Is Wood" in Volume 26, starting on page 3261. You'll find information about use of pressure-treated lumber in fence construction in Volume 9, page 1142. The information there applies to any outdoor construction project using this kind of lumber. Using redwood in outdoor projects is covered in some detail in the article about redwood decks in Volume 7, page 783.

Additional detail about composting and composters is in the article about gardening in Volume 11.

Other coldframe plans are in Volume 11 of the *Encyclopedia*, beginning on page 1354. Hotbed plans are in that same volume, beginning on page 1357.

You'll find detailed plans for building a cloche and other gardening aids in Volume 11, beginning on page 1362.

Wooden seed flats are simple to make in your workshop and will last for years.

Three different greenhouse projects are described in detail in Volume 11, beginning on page 1378. One of these, a greenhouse that fits in a window, is easily adapted to homes with limited yard space. Plans for a solar garden shed are in Volume 22, beginning on page 2768.

Before you start any fencing project for your garden, be sure to check Volume 9 of the Popular Mechanics *Do-it-Yourself Encyclopedia*. Beginning on page 1133, you'll find many helpful hints and actual building projects for a wide variety of fences using many different fencing materials.

There are plans for potting benches in Volume 3 page 309, and more in Volume 11 on page 1361.

Garden planters are the topic of an article beginning on page 2258 in Volume 18, while patio planters are covered in Volume 17 beginning on page 2158.

Outdoor structure projects are also in the *Do-it-Yourself Encyclopedia*. Garden sheds are the topic of an article in Volume 27, beginning on page 3441, and plans for a garden work center are in that same volume, beginning on page 3438.

Throughout the 27 volumes of the Popular Mechanics *Do-it-Yourself Encyclopedia*, you'll find tips and detailed construction articles that will stimulate more of your own ideas about garden projects—from selecting the correct nails and screws to knowing more about lumber and wood products.

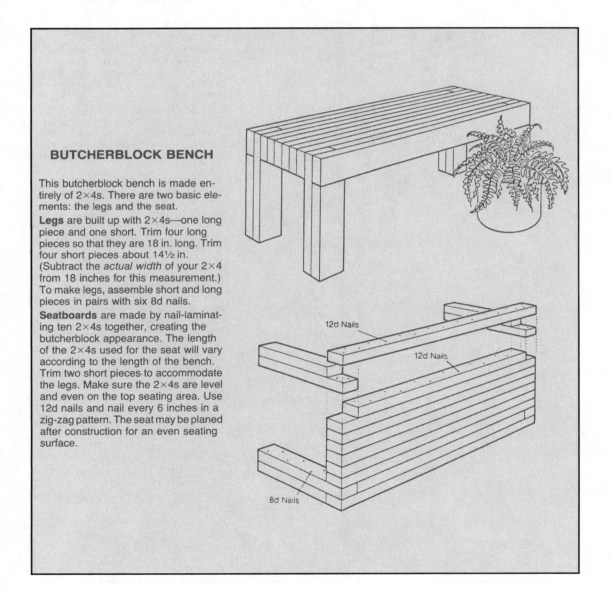

BUTCHERBLOCK BENCH

This butcherblock bench is made entirely of 2×4s. There are two basic elements: the legs and the seat.

Legs are built up with 2×4s—one long piece and one short. Trim four long pieces so that they are 18 in. long. Trim four short pieces about 14½ in. (Subtract the *actual width* of your 2×4 from 18 inches for this measurement.) To make legs, assemble short and long pieces in pairs with six 8d nails.

Seatboards are made by nail-laminating ten 2×4s together, creating the butcherblock appearance. The length of the 2×4s used for the seat will vary according to the length of the bench. Trim two short pieces to accommodate the legs. Make sure the 2×4s are level and even on the top seating area. Use 12d nails and nail every 6 inches in a zig-zag pattern. The seat may be planed after construction for an even seating surface.

12d Nails

12d Nails

8d Nails

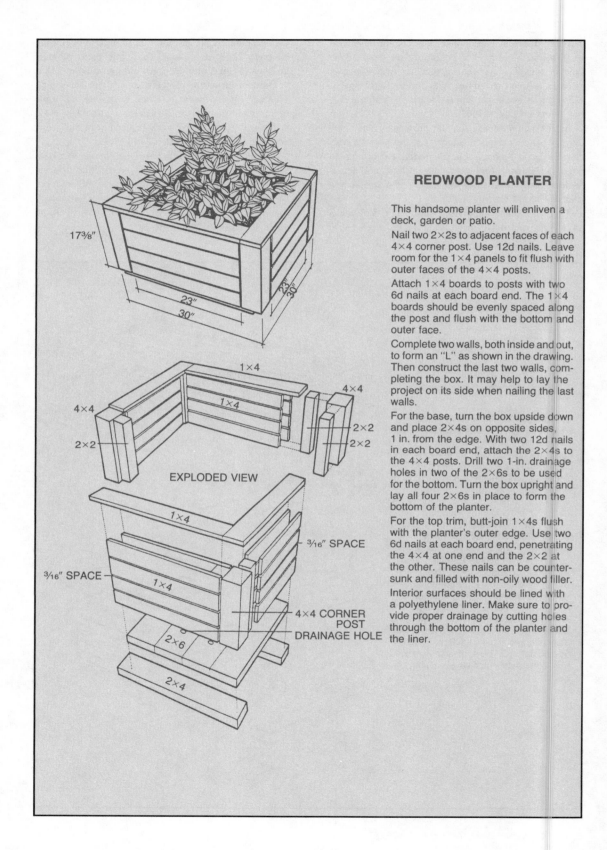

17³⁄₈"

23"

30"

1×4

4×4

4×4

2×2

2×2

2×2

2×2

EXPLODED VIEW

1×4

³⁄₁₆" SPACE

³⁄₁₆" SPACE

1×4

4×4 CORNER POST

2×6

DRAINAGE HOLE

2×4

REDWOOD PLANTER

This handsome planter will enliven a deck, garden or patio.

Nail two 2×2s to adjacent faces of each 4×4 corner post. Use 12d nails. Leave room for the 1×4 panels to fit flush with outer faces of the 4×4 posts.

Attach 1×4 boards to posts with two 6d nails at each board end. The 1×4 boards should be evenly spaced along the post and flush with the bottom and outer face.

Complete two walls, both inside and out, to form an "L" as shown in the drawing. Then construct the last two walls, completing the box. It may help to lay the project on its side when nailing the last walls.

For the base, turn the box upside down and place 2×4s on opposite sides, 1 in. from the edge. With two 12d nails in each board end, attach the 2×4s to the 4×4 posts. Drill two 1-in. drainage holes in two of the 2×6s to be used for the bottom. Turn the box upright and lay all four 2×6s in place to form the bottom of the planter.

For the top trim, butt-join 1×4s flush with the planter's outer edge. Use two 6d nails at each board end, penetrating the 4×4 at one end and the 2×2 at the other. These nails can be countersunk and filled with non-oily wood filler.

Interior surfaces should be lined with a polyethylene liner. Make sure to provide proper drainage by cutting holes through the bottom of the planter and the liner.

5

Soil Types and Treatments

You will know good soil when you get your hands on it. Good soil crumbles easily, holds water well and does not clump up when being worked.

Types of Soil

Your garden can have any one or a combination of three basic soil types: clay, sandy or loam.

Clay is heavy and dense. While it is high in mineral content, it doesn't contain much oxygen or permit good drainage. Root development for young plants is difficult in this type of soil. Clay forms a hard clod when dry and feels slightly greasy when wet.

Sandy soil is a good planting medium because it does not clump up, it drains quickly and can be worked early in the season. Unfortunately, sandy soil, because of its porosity, does not hold moisture well and valuable nutrients are lost quickly.

Loam is the type of garden soil everyone strives for. This is a combination of clay, sand and organic material. It drains well but not too quickly, contains generous amounts of organic material and is easily worked.

Soil amendments include anything you add to the soil to improve its condition. Any garden will benefit dramatically when you add soil amendments on a regular basis. Compost is the best additive you can give your soil. Peat moss is another good conditioner that will increase the overall quality of the soil. Commercial fertilizers are common inorganic amendments used to increase specific soil nutrient elements.

Soil Testing

You should test your soil regularly to determine its acidity or alkalinity. You should also test the levels of nitrogen, phosphorus and potassium. Based on the analysis of your test results, you'll know how much and what kind of conditioners and fertilizers to add to develop a perfectly balanced growing medium.

You can do your own soil testing with an inexpensive kit, or you can bring a sample to your agricultural extension agent. The first test should be to find out the pH level of the soil.

Soil pH. The pH level is a measure of how acid or alkaline a given sample of soil is. The pH balance affects the solubility of important nutrients and helps the plant regulate its metabolism and nutrient uptake.

The scale for measuring pH runs from 0 to 14 with 7 being neutral. A pH below 7.0 is acid; a pH above 7.0 is alkaline. Most vegetables will grow well in soil that is just below neutral and slightly acid—6.5 to 6.8 pH.

Once you've determined the pH of your soil, you can add agricultural sulfur to lower the pH or raise the pH by adding ground limestone. Peat moss is also acidic and adding it to your soil will lower the pH level.

Soil Nutrients. You must also test to determine the levels of three important soil nutrients: nitrogen, phosphorus and potassium, or as they are commonly called, N-P-K.

Nitrogen (N) promotes rapid growth and dark green foliage. This nutrient is especially important for plants whose leaves are harvested—lettuce, spinach, Swiss chard, kale and collards. Nitrogen is a common element. About 80% of our atmosphere is nitrogen, but most plants can't use this form of free

Test your own garden soil with a soil testing kit.

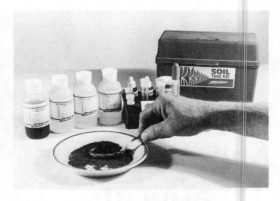

To test soil pH, begin by pulverizing soil sample.

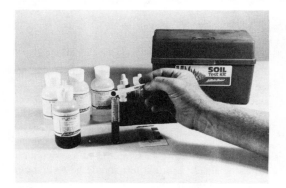

Add soil to pH indicating solution in a test tube.

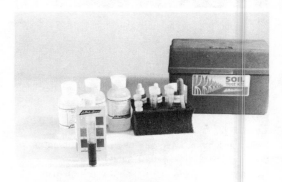

Compare solution color of tested soil to pH chart.

nitrogen. A large group of plants called **legumes** do, however, have the ability to convert atmospheric nitrogen into a usable form. Some of the most common types of legumes include soybeans, alfalfa, peanuts and peas. Sources of nitrogen for other kinds of plants come from the application of commercial nitrogen fertilizers and from well decomposed organic materials such as compost in the soil. As organic material *begins* to decompose, however, the microorganisms use a lot of nitrogen that might cause a temporary deficiency in the soil.

Phosphorus (P), in the form of sulfate of potash, is important for root growth. It aids in the production of fruit and flowers and helps plants develop sturdiness.

Potassium (K) offers a balance between the growth factor of nitrogen and the ripening influence of phosphorus. It is necessary for new cell growth, especially for root and bulb crops such as carrots, potatoes and beets.

In addition to the three main nutrients required for sound plant growth and development, good soil also needs several secondary nutrients: magnesium (Mg), calcium (Ca) and sulfur (S). Other plant nutrients, carbon (C), hydrogen (H) and oxygen (O), come from atmospheric carbon dioxide and from water.

Chemical Fertilizers

Fertilizers come in many different types and forms. Any fertilizer which contains all three primary nutrient elements—nitrogen, phosphorus and potassium (N-P-K)—is considered a **complete fertilizer**. Fertilizers must have a guaranteed analysis of their chemical makeup with the percentage of the three primary elements stated on the label. For example, a garden fertilizer labeled 5-10-5 contains 5% nitrogen, 10% phosphorus and 5% potassium. The remaining material (80% in this example) is filler or contains just trace amounts of other nutrients.

You can buy fertilizers in several formulations such as soluble, granule, time-release, pellets and stakes. You mix a soluble fertilizer with water before being applied when watering, irrigating or spraying. Granule, time-release and pellets are commonly broadcast over an area, then worked into the soil.

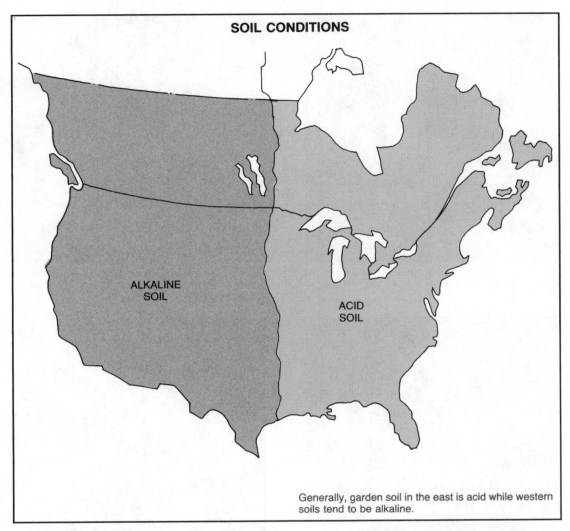

SOIL CONDITIONS

ALKALINE
SOIL

ACID
SOIL

Generally, garden soil in the east is acid while western
soils tend to be alkaline.

Stakes are pounded into the ground around trees or plants and their fertilizer is released over time during normal watering.

Organic Fertilizers

Besides chemical fertilizers there are many organic sources of the three major nutrients.

Good organic sources of nitrogen include: cotton-seed meal, fish meal, blood meal and horn meal. For phosphorus use bonemeal, phosphate rock and soft phosphate. Organic sources of potash include kelp meal, wood ashes, crushed granite and green-sand.

Humus

Humus provides a moist, nutrient-rich condition for roots to grow. Roots don't grow *in* soil but rather in the spaces *between* particles of soil. In some soil these spaces are too large, and the plant is deprived

of enough moisture and support. In other soil the particles are packed too tightly, inhibiting root growth.

Humus in sandy soil binds the particles together to help retain moisture longer. In clay, humus keeps the soil particles separated allowing room for air and water to enter. "Rich" soils have a lot of humus; "lean" soils have less, maybe even a deficiency in the conditions humus provides.

Humus is a natural material made from decomposed plant and animal wastes. Common sources of humus for the garden are grass clippings, fallen leaves, sawdust, animal manure and even kitchen scraps. Decomposition is necessary for any of the nutrients in humus to be taken up by the plant. These materials, however, decompose very slowly if left alone. You can buy peat moss from garden supply centers to help organic waste decompose faster.

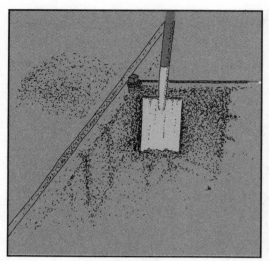

Dig a trench, about 18 inches wide, halfway down the garden row. Pile soil outside the bed near the middle of the plot.

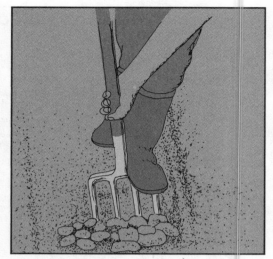

Break up the bottom of the trench with a spading fork and work humus into the trench bottom. Work the humus in evenly.

Dig another strip, turning the soil upside down in the open trench. It is easier to dig the soil from the open side of a trench.

Work across half the plot, then work your way back for the other half. Use the first pile of soil to fill the last trench in the plot.

In the process of decomposing, the material uses large amounts of nitrogen, robbing the soil of this needed nutrient. One way to reslove this problem is to compost the material, giving it the place and conditions to decompose away from the working soil of your garden.

Compost

Well-aged compost is a soft, crumbly brown that is the result of decaying plant and vegetable matter. Compost has some value as a plant food and for improving the overall texture of soil, but its greatest value is in supplying soil with moisture-holding humus.

It makes good sense for you to recycle garden refuse such as weeds, grass clippings and spent plants. First, the average garden will generate hundreds of pounds of this waste material every season. Piling this in one area to decompose is much easier than hauling it to the dump.

Of greater importance is the finished product, compost. Adding compost will make any soil lighter, increase its ability to hold moisture and provide a more ideal growing medium for plants.

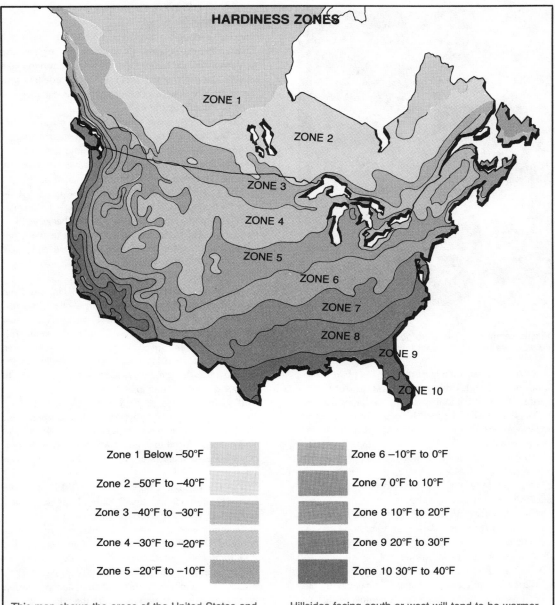

HARDINESS ZONES

ZONE 1
ZONE 2
ZONE 3
ZONE 4
ZONE 5
ZONE 6
ZONE 7
ZONE 8
ZONE 9
ZONE 10

Zone 1 Below –50°F

Zone 2 –50°F to –40°F

Zone 3 –40°F to –30°F

Zone 4 –30°F to –20°F

Zone 5 –20°F to –10°F

Zone 6 –10°F to 0°F

Zone 7 0°F to 10°F

Zone 8 10°F to 20°F

Zone 9 20°F to 30°F

Zone 10 30°F to 40°F

This map shows the areas of the United States and Canada that have similar conditions for plant growth and survival, based on the minimum winter temperatures expected. These hardiness zones can give you a general idea of how well certain types of plants in your garden will survive from season to season. Use it as a general guide to select plants for your garden.

For example, plants that thrive in Zone 9 in southern Texas and Georgia may also do well along the coastal regions of Oregon and British Columbia.

These zones give you only a general reference. There are other climate and environmental factors you should consider for your specific area.

Hillsides facing south or west will tend to be warmer than slopes facing north or east. Areas along a lake or coastline usually have more moderate temperatures than inland areas. Urban areas, with heat-holding concrete and buildings have a warmer climate for gardening than rural areas in the same Zone. Hilltops tend to be a harsher climate for gardens than valleys that are protected from winds that make it colder in winter and drier in summer.

Consider other plant growth factors when you determine the type of plants suitable for your area. Frost, rainfall, humidity, soil characteristics and sun exposure may have little relationship to the average winter temperatures used to determine these Zones of Hardiness.

Plastic composting bin looks good in the garden and helps make usable compost fast.

Since compost is made from decaying plant matter, it not only provides the major conditions for healthy gardens but also contains many of the important trace nutrients as well. The N-P-K values of compost are low, however, and you should add fertilizer for optimum growth.

All you need to make good compost is refuse, water and air.

Organic refuse is the basis of a compost pile and this is available around the lawn and garden. Organic kitchen refuse, such as fruit and vegetable peelings and coffee grounds, is another good additive to your compost pile. Don't add meat, bones or pet droppings. These materials do not decay well and give off a putrid odor.

Water is another key element to the decaying process. It is important to keep your compost pile damp. To ensure the right moisture content, wet down each layer of material as it is applied. During dry weather, wet down the pile every two days.

Air circulation is also important to a good compost pile. Turn the pile frequently—at least every other week—to speed up the decaying process. By turning the compost pile often, the outer edges which tend to dry out quickly are turned inward toward the center of the pile and you let more oxygen enter.

Composters

Making a compost pile is simple. You can stack layers of organic waste in an open area or you can buy sophisticated tumbler drums which claim to make usable compost in two weeks. Most gardeners will agree however, that composting is easiest in some type of bin arrangement.

Commercially-made polypropylene plastic cylinders and bins are designed to aid in the making of compost. These are attractive, durable and efficient to use. The do-it-yourselfer can save substantially by making rather than buying a composter.

Part of the trick of making compost quickly is to shred organic materials before adding to the pile. Shredded materials decompose faster because there is much more surface area for bacteria to work on. A garden shredder is ideal for this. You can make compost without a shredder, but it will take longer for the organic material to decompose.

Begin by making a pile 8 in. to 10 in. high out of grass clippings, garden trimmings, plants, leaves, kitchen scraps and other organic waste. Add a few cups of ground limestone or a layer of manure followed by a 2-in. layer of garden soil. Wet down the pile with a garden hose. Build all layers in the compost pile the same way, always finishing off with a layer of soil to contain odors.

If your lawn has been treated with weed killers, **do not** add these grass clippings to the compost pile. The chemicals in weed killers are long-lived and will not be reduced in strength when the grass decomposes. The residual weed killers can damage your garden.

The top of your compost pile should be concave rather than mounded up. This will prevent water runoff and will help keep the pile damp.

Depending on the size of the material you use as compost, it will take from 2 to 12 months for the pile to decompose completely. As decomposition takes place, heat will be generated—120°F to 180°F, in fact. Once the heat starts to subside, decomposition is slowing down and you must turn the pile. A garden thermometer will indicate the current state of heat generation and let you know when you should turn the pile.

The most difficult part of making good compost is turning the pile, simply because you must lift hundreds of pounds of material. The best tool for turning compost is a pitch fork. Work carefully, lifting only as much material as you can handle easily to reduce the possibility of back strain.

Mulch

Mulch is a soil cover that creates better growing and soil conditions for your plants. Mulch is put on top of the soil; compost is worked into the soil. Your garden is mulched naturally when dead leaves, twigs and plants fall to the ground. A layer of mulch around garden plants helps preserve the moisture in the soil. It's also good for discouraging weed growth.

Mulch improves the quality of both clay and sandy soils. It prevents compacting in heavier soils like clay. It can help looser sandy soils retain moisture longer. It also keeps rain from splashing up under leaves, controlling somewhat the spread of fungus.

Natural mulch is organic material such as leaves, hay or grass clippings. Hay that has already begun to decompose is better than fresh. Grass clippings should have begun to dry and turn gray. Leaves that are dry and broken up will provide a better mulch than freshly-fallen leaves. Sawdust, wood chips and pine needles also make good mulch because they hold moisture.

Commercial mulch like peat moss and pine bark chips can be purchased at a garden supply center. You can also buy black plastic mulch, often sold in strips, to place around plants much the same way you do with natural mulch materials. Plastic mulch, of course, does not decompose but it does provide quick soil protection and heat-conserving conditions for plants set out in the early spring.

A layer of mulch on the soil year round will keep the soil at a more constant temperature—it will take longer for it to warm up and cool down.

Water

Water is important to all plants. Seeds need water to germinate and plants send out a root system to collect it as they grow. Water makes up more than 80% of the weight of a living plant. It dissolves nutrients in the soil, letting the roots absorb the solution.

You can kill plants by overwatering. The danger comes from the buildup of free water in the soil. When water fills the spaces between soil particles, the supply of oxygen is cut off from the roots and the plant begins to drown. The type of soil you have will determine how much free water it will hold. Sandy soils drain quickly; clay soils are slow to drain; loam drains somewhere in between.

Underwatering can result in poor plant growth. When soil is not watered deeply enough, the root systems find water close to the surface, resulting in a shallow, underdeveloped system.

Most gardens need about 1 in. of water per week, though raised-bed gardens in the more arid parts will require up to 2 in. per week. Where natural rainfall is heavy, less watering is necessary. Let common sense be your guide. Scrape away a few inches of soil to see if it is damp or moist. If soil is dry a few inches down, water heavily to bring it to the desired level.

You can tell how much water your garden is receiving by placing several empty coffee cans around the plot. When each of the cans has an inch of water in it—through normal sprinkling or rain—stop watering. Adjust your watering to suit local conditions.

Foliar feeding of plants is simple with a power sprayer.

Shredded materials convert into compost faster than organic materials in a natural state.

6

Controlling Pests

Among all the beauty and wonder of warm weather, there is also the threat of attack on your garden from a variety of living things. An evening's work by a few hungry slugs can easily take a big bite out of your small lettuce patch. A little over-zealous watering can create a fungus problem on your plants.

Types of Pests

Your first job is to recognize the pests you need to control. For your purposes in gardening, pests can be insects, vertebrates, weeds and plant diseases.

Insects thrive in more environments than any other group of living things. There are about 800,000 different insects on our planet. In fact, the insect kingdom is the largest of all. Of these, 99% are beneficial or not harmful to humans or plant life. Many beneficial insects eat harmful insects. Wasps, for example, find aphids a tasty treat. Bees are also valuable because they cross-pollinate vegetable and fruit flowers in the normal course of their daily activities. Earthworms pass tons of soil through their bodies during their lifetime. Their tunneling action helps break up soil and aids in the introduction of oxygen.

Vertebrates are animals with a jointed backbone. They include, among others, snakes, birds and small animals. What may be a pest in some situations may be a welcomed animal in others. Most of the vertebrates cause little permanent damage in the garden and are usually easily controlled.

Weeds are simply plants out of place. They reduce the yields in your garden by competing with your crops and flowers for soil nutrients and moisture. Some can even cause you more direct problems through skin irritations or allergies.

Plant diseases are any harmful conditions that make a plant different from normal in the way it looks or in the way it functions. Some plant diseases are caused by non-living things such as extreme temperatures, nutrient deficiencies, lack of water or injury to the plant. Other diseases are caused by living organisms that live and feed on the plant. Some of the more common of this kind of plant diseases are fungi, bacteria, viruses and nematodes.

Types of Controls

Pesticides are products that eliminate or control any type of animal, insect or plant disease in the garden.

In our struggle against garden pests, we often just use the handiest or cheapest pesticide—usually an inorganic chemical product. We often forget to consider other methods or the effects on the environment. Some people feel there are enough poisons in our soil, water and atmosphere. They will not contribute one speck more, at least as far as possible. To solve pest problems responsibly, you must know what control methods are available and then evaluate the benefits and risks of each. This will let you choose the most effective method and cause the least harm to you and the environment.

Study all your options to control pests in the garden. It is not always necessary to drench soil and plants with toxic substances to control insects or diseases.

There are three basic types of control for pests in the family garden: physical, biological, and chemical.

Physical controls are one way of getting rid of pests. You can put up barriers to divert them and keep things tidy, depriving pests of an attractive environment. You can also capture or lure insects or small animals into traps where they die or are released away from the garden and out of harm's way.

Biological control is a common way to handle insects and some weeds. This involves releasing natural enemies such as parasites, predators and disease agents into the pest's environment.

Chemical controls involve the use of pesticides in the form of sprays, powders, granules, and baits to solve both insect and disease problems. The final decision to use chemical controls on your garden is a personal one.

PHYSICAL CONTROLS

Physical controls are necessary for all gardens to prevent damage to growing plants. Often they are intended not only to prevent damage by insects and small animals but also to deter other forces working against you in your garden.

Fencing

It has been said that good fences make good neighbors, and this also applies to gardening. If you live in a rural area, your garden can become a meal ticket for a variety of animals like deer and raccoons unless it is adequately fenced. People in urban areas should also consider fencing to keep out dogs, cats and unruly neighborhood children.

Fencing is a good example of physical control that works well for small gardens.

Effective fencing materials include chainlink, barbed wire and chicken wire. Open mesh is better than solid board fencing because it does not shade the garden.

Fencing will not keep out rodents, birds or insects. For these pests, there are other physical controls.

Barriers and Scare Tactics

Fruits and berries are a favorite food of birds. You can lose a large portion of your crop unless some type of physical control deters them. Cover small fruit trees and berry bushes with netting available from garden centers and hardware stores. To protect trees too large to cover, hang plastic bottles from branches. Cut two flaps on opposite sides of the bottles. When the wind blows, the bottle will spin and scare off birds. Mirrors or aluminum foil suspended to reflect light patterns will also frighten birds. A scarecrow can sometimes scare off larger birds such as crows and ravens, although some of these crafty birds have become so urbanized they befriend the scarecrow!

Traps are probably the best way of catching rodents in the garden.

Traps

Small animals such as mice, moles and gophers can do much damage. When you see evidence of them in the garden—most commonly by a dirt mound or raised dirt over a tunnel—you should take steps to eliminate them. The most effective means is trapping, even though there are also chemical and gas treatments available. Many gardeners have successfully scared away moles by simply pushing a wind-activated noisemaker through the soil into the tunnel. The vibrations get rid of moles from yards and gardens in just a couple of days.

Hand Removal

An effective physical control for insects is just to pick them off the plants. This control works well for worms, slugs, caterpillars and many beetles. If you're squeamish, use surgical hemostats, tweezers or pliers to pick up these pests. Then, drop them into a small container half-filled with kerosene. If you prefer to let them live out their lives feeding on wild plants, you can also deposit them in wooded areas far enough away from your garden so they won't migrate back. While you will not catch all the insects by hand, you can remove quite a few of the slow movers and heavy eaters.

To capture insects such as slugs and earwigs, put boards at different places around the garden. These pests are active at night and hide from sunlight. During the day, lift up a board and you'll usually find a few of these insects; just pick them up and get rid of them.

Companion Planting

Companion planting is another physical control you can use. Some plants, such as multiplier onions, garlic, basil and marigolds are all good choices. When you plant these by vegetables, they will deter light insect infestations.

Water Pressure and Soaps

The simplest, safest form of insect control can be periodic treatment with a strong spray from a garden hose. This is an effective control for aphids. Stronger controls are insecticidal soaps and citrus oil sprays. Insecticidal soaps and oil sprays are quick acting, biodegradable and not harmful to people, livestock, pets, honeybees or other beneficial insects such as the praying mantis or ladybug.

BIOLOGICAL CONTROLS

As an alternative to physical or chemical controls, the environmentally-conscious gardener can control garden pests biologically.

Bacteriological Controls

Biological control for specific insects such as Japanese beetle grubs, grasshoppers and crickets involves introduction of bacteria which attack these insects. Research and development of bacteriological controls is a growing field. Here are two examples:

Japanese Beetle Control. Japanese beetles, first discovered in the United States around 1916, have spread throughout much of the country. They are also found in Quebec and Ontario, particularly in some urban areas. Check with your agricultural extension agent to see if Japanese beetles are considered

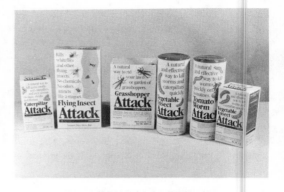

Many safe sprays are available if you don't want to use toxic chemicals.

a problem in your area, although it will be obvious to you when you have a serious infestation.

Adult beetles attack more than 275 different kinds of trees, shrubs, turf, field crops and garden crops. Immature grubs feed on roots and underground stems of plants, particularly grasses, and can easily become an infestation. Commercial losses to these insects amount to millions of dollars annually.

Both the adult and grub Japanese beetles can be controlled by chemical means, but you can also use biological controls. The grubs are subject to diseases, one of which is known as **milky spore disease**. Milky spore does not infect plants or other insects, birds and warm blooded animals. In time, however, applications of milky spore will help wipe out Japanese beetle grubs.

Milky spore bacteria are tiny. Five thousand of these spores placed end to end would make a line only about an inch long. You apply these spores mixed with a filler material such as talc or chalk to a lawn or garden area. Japanese beetle grubs burrow through the soil, feeding on roots of plants and take in the spores. The spores germinate inside the grubs and multiply rapidly in their blood.

While some diseases will kill insects quickly, milky spores take time. Infected grubs may live for months, particularly if temperatures are low. Infected grubs may, in fact, live until spring (when infected late in the fall) but will not develop into adult Japanese beetles. When infected grubs die, they release millions of new spores into the soil. These are eaten by other grubs who die and release more of the bacteria. The more grubs present, the faster the spores will spread throughout the lawn or garden area. You must allow time for infection to begin and for the grubs to die.

You'll get a more complete and permanent control if all your neighbors join you in the milky spore treatment. The adult Japanese beetle, emigrating from

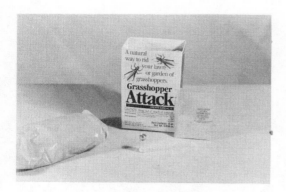

An effective control for grasshoppers is *nosema locus-tae* spores which infect only members of the *Melano-plus* family of insects—grasshoppers and crickets.

your neighbor's yard, will not stop at your treated lot line as it flies to find a tasty meal on your roses. Some commercial applicators of milky spore will guarantee results for 7 to 10 years if the entire neighborhood is treated. They often give quantity discounts to do an entire area.

Grasshopper and Cricket Control.

Control grasshoppers and crickets with an application of *nosema locustae* spores, a natural microbial insecticide. When used as directed, this protozoan spore provides a long-term control, with optimum benefits by the second season.

Nosema locustae spores are mixed with bran meal, a favored food of grasshoppers and crickets. As the treated bran is eaten, the nosema spores germinate in the midgut and penetrate into the insect's body. The infection spreads and more spores are produced. The insect becomes lethargic, decreases feeding, and reduces its reproduction activity. Weakened by the bacteria, grasshoppers fall prey to stronger members who also become infected and spread the spores. When applied according to directions, you can expect a 50% mortality rate within 3 to 4 months, with 35% to 50% of the survivors infected. This natural biological control is safe to use and has no harmful effects on humans, domesticated animals, fish or other similar life forms.

Biological Traps

Biological traps are also useful for home gardeners. Some release a scent, usually a sex lure, that attracts specific male insects. Once the male insect enters, he is held by a sticky substance and dies. Other traps are brightly colored, attracting insects to a sticky surface, much like flypaper. Traps are available for the gypsy moth, Japanese beetle, fruit fly, cabbage looper, corn earworm, European corn borer, fall armyworm, grape berry moth, codling moth, leafroller

moth, oriental fruit moth, orange tortrix and the spruce budworm.

You should also inspect the traps to find out what types of insects are in the area and when infestations are on the rise. You'll find this helpful for timing spray programs or other insect control measures. Empty the traps periodically. Insects will be repelled by the odor of dead bodies. Most traps have a life of about one growing season, but you may need to rebait some traps several times during the season. Check them every couple of days. Traps are also useful for catching insects in food storage areas such as a root cellar.

One word of caution about biological traps. They work best if you have a heavy concentration of the pest population. If your infestation is light, the lure of the scent may attract more insects to your yard or garden than you had before you started the control. If you aren't careful, Japanese beetle traps will be especially effective in transferring your neighbor's insect problem to your yard.

Beneficial insects are an effective control for some insect problems.

Control by Natural Enemies

Birds eat insects so attracting birds to your garden would look like an effective control. But birds are just as fond of corn, most stone fruits and berries. Likewise, snakes eat rodents, but most gardeners would rather use a spring trap than introduce snakes to control a rodent problem.

Introducing beneficial insects is an effective biological control. These include ladybugs, praying mantis, green lacewings and fly parasites. You can often buy these beneficial insects at a garden center.

Beneficial insects eat harmful insects and are effective and safe as a control. Timing of release is important; if there are too few pest insects available, the beneficial insects will fly to other areas. Suppliers suggest two or three releases per season for best results.

Traps, which contain pheromone, an insect sex lure, are effective for controlling insects.

Power sprayers are useful for a variety of spraying and power washing tasks in the garden.

CHEMICAL CONTROLS

Chemical use in the garden carries a special responsibility. Follow label cautions and directions carefully. Remember, storage, use and disposal of any chemical is potentially dangerous.

Pesticides

Pesticides are chemical controls for all types of plant diseases and garden pests. The most common in gardening are insecticides and fungicides, but you can get specialized pesticide products to solve any garden problem. A list of common types of pesticides is included in this chapter.

Using Pesticides

You can use pesticide products effectively if you follow some basic guidelines. Some insecticides require a waiting period of up to 14 days between spraying and harvesting vegetables. Others can be sprayed on your crop within a day of harvesting. Check the container label for the **residual toxicity** of the insecticide or fungicide you are using. This tells you how long the harmful effect of the chemical will last on the plant or in the soil.

Types of Formulations

You can buy pesticide products as dusts, granules, baits, concentrated solutions (which must be diluted before use) and ready-to-use sprays commonly sold in pump spray bottles and aerosol cans.

Sprays. These formulations are liquids with the active ingredient in solution with a solvent. Most aerosol spray cans have a low percentage of active ingredient.

Baits. A bait formulation is an edible or attractive substance mixed with a pesticide. The bait attracts the pests and the pesticide kills them. Use baits to control rodents and insects.

Dusts. Dusts for tomatoes, roses and vegetables are an effective way to control insects and some plant diseases. Dusts may contain malathion, rotenone and carbaryl by themselves or in some combination. Usually the container is also a sprayer for applying the dust. Apply only late in the day when the air is still and when bees are not active. Most dusts will kill bees. You might want to look for dusts that contain one or more fungicides like captan as well as insecticides.

Granules. Granular formulations are dry. They are most often used as soil treatments, applied either directly to the soil or over the plants. Granules are safer to apply than dusts because there is less chance of chemical drift in the wind. Granular formulations are available to combat insects, diseases and unwanted plants (such as crabgrass).

Soluble Powders. These are dry formulations that are added to water to make a solution. In most cases, you'll have to keep the applicator stirred or shaken to keep the powder dissolved.

PESTICIDE PRODUCTS

Pesticide products like herbicides, some fungicides and plant growth regulators, are designed to be used at different times in the growing season.

Preemergence pesticide products are used before crops or weeds emerge. They can also be used after crops emerge or are established but before weeds emerge.

Preplant pesticide products are used before the crop is planted.

Postemergence pesticide products are used after the crop or weeds have emerged.

What Pesticides to Use

In choosing a control to use for insects or plant diseases, remember some pesticides have been taken off the market, and more are banned each year. Some are illegal to use in one area, but the same product may be sold in other places. New safer products appear on the market annually as well. Here is a description of the most popular types of biological and chemical insect and plant disease controls.

Antibiotics are used to control bacterial diseases in plants. Some of the more popular antibiotics include streptomycin, cycloheximide and chlortetracycline.

Bacillus thuringiensis (B-T) is a biological control for bagworms, cankerworms, gypsy moth and tent caterpillars. It's harmless to humans and animals. It comes in either a dust or a spray under such trade names as Attack, Biotrol, Dipel, Safer or Thurcide.

Bordeau mixture is a water suspension of copper and lime. It is sold under a variety of trade names. It is commonly used in heavy concentration as a dormant spray.

TYPES OF PESTICIDE PRODUCTS

Pesticide products are chemicals used to destroy or control pests. They also include chemicals used to regulate plant growth and control plant diseases. Here are the types and uses of pesticide products:

Acaricides control mites, ticks and spiders.

Antitranspirants coat the leaves of plants to reduce unwanted water loss.

Attractants lure pests.

Avicides control birds.

Bactericides control bacteria.

Defoliants remove unwanted plant growth without killing the plant immediately.

Desiccants dry up plant leaves and stems and insects.

Fungicides control fungi.

Herbicides control weeds.

Insecticides control insects and other pests such as ticks and spiders.

Miticides are used to control mites.

Molluscicides control mollusks such as slugs and snails.

Nematicides control nematodes.

Piscides control fish

Plant growth regulators stop, speed up or change normal plant processes.

Predacides control vertebrate pests.

Repellents keep pests away.

Rodenticides control rodents.

Captan is an organic fungicide used to control all types of fungus diseases. You can use it to control black spot on roses. It is also used to coat seeds that are slow to germinate (such as corn, peas and potatoes), so they don't rot before emerging. Captan can also treat spring and summer flowering bulbs such as tulips and gladiolus.

Carbaryl, for the control of Japanese beetles and European corn borer, is commonly marketed under the name Sevin. Carbaryl is especially lethal for honey bees; it must be used sparingly and late in the day when the bees are not active.

Diazinon is a broad-spectrum insecticide sold under many trade names, such as Spectracide or Gardentox. Diazinon can be sprayed or worked directly into the soil. It has a 14-day minimum residual toxicity, which means you can't harvest treated vegetables for at least two weeks. It is also an effective control for soil insects that attack root crops. Dilute according to label directions and soak the soil after plants emerge. Additional applications may be necessary during the growing season if you see continued evidence of damage.

Folpet is a wettable powder or dust fungicide that is similar to captan and sold under the trade name Phaltan. It can be used on fruits, flowers, vegetables and trees.

Insecticidal soap is a very safe mixture of potassium soap. Use it for control of piercing or sucking insects like aphids. It's safe enough to use indoors on house plants. Insecticidal soap is safe for fruits and vegetables and can be applied the same day you harvest with no residual toxicity.

Malathion, another broad-spectrum insecticide, has a residual toxicity of 7 days, so it *should not* be sprayed close to harvest time. It provides effective control of Mexican bean beetles and leaf miners.

Maneb is a wettable powder or dust fungicide sold under the names Dithane M-22, Manzate and Dithane S-31. It is used to control rust, leaf spots, scab, coryneum blight and gray mold. It is very popular for use on roses.

Rotenone-pyrethrum are two insecticides commonly sold in combination. Both ingredients are organic and fairly safe to use. They help get rid of aphids, leaf miners, Mexican bean beetles and whiteflies. Pyrethrum does kill bees, however, and it should not be used when bees are active.

Sulfur can be used as a fungicide to control apple scab and powdery mildew on trees and small fruits. It comes as a dust or spray from many manufacturers.

Zineb is a fungicide used to control a wide range of diseases on vegetables, fruits and ornamental plants. One of the many trade names under which zineb is sold is Dithane Z-78.

Product Ineffectiveness

Many times you may not get the desired results with pesticide products. The problem may not always be the fault of the product, but could be the result of other conditions affecting control.

Pesticide resistance is one condition affecting control. Rarely does any pesticide kill all the target pests. Each time a pesticide is used, it selectively kills the most sensitive pests. Some pests avoid the control. Others are able to withstand its effect. Pests that are not controlled pass along to their offspring the trait that allowed them to survive.

Pest immunity can develop when you use one pesticide product repeatedly in the same place. The pest population builds up a natural resistance to it. Some insects have become practically immune to control by certain pesticides, and repeated applications have done nothing but increase risks to humans. This is why DDT has been taken off the market.

Incorrect application may be another reason to account for control failure. You may have used the wrong product; the dosage may have not been correct, or you could have applied the pesticide incorrectly.

Organic matter in soil also limits pesticide activity, especially when the product is being used to control plant diseases. Soils with a lot of organic matter may need higher rates of application. Soil texture also affects the way pesticides work. Soils with fine particles (like you find in clay) may need higher application rates. Coarser soils, like sand, have less surface area and you should lower application rates.

Soil moisture and rain affect the way pesticide products work. They also affect how long the pesticides stay on soil and plants. Control with products like herbicides is best with moderate soil moisture. Heavy moisture content may keep the chemical from contacting the soil particles. On the other hand, because herbicides work best when plants are growing fast, you want conditions of high humidity and optimum temperatures that cause this rapid growth.

Rain is good when you apply preemergence controls to the surface. It carries the control down into the soil to the pests. But rain during or soon after a surface or foliar application is not good. It may wash the product off the leaves.

Chemical Control Cautions

Chemical controls with some pesticide products can cause injury to humans, animals and beneficial insects because they are toxic. But these same controls can be effective and safe in your garden if used safely, according to manufacturer's label directions, and stored properly. Give any chemical control you use in the garden the same cautious respect you give any toxic substance.

Children under 10 are the victims of at least half the accidental pesticide deaths. If pesticides were always cared for correctly, children would never touch them.

Here are a few suggestions about safe application and storage of chemical controls.

● DO store and use chemicals away from children.

● DO take care to read and follow all label directions when using any chemical pesticide.

● DO protect yourself when using chemical insecticides by wearing clothing that covers your arms and legs, face mask (with filter), eye protection, gloves, waterproof footwear and a hat to protect your scalp.

● DO protect others when spraying by keeping children, pets and others away from the area.

● DO adjust spray equipment to operate properly. Clean all equipment after use according to manufacturers' instructions.

● DO spray when the weather is dry.

● DO follow product label directions. If you have any questions, ask—either at the store or from the manufacturer of the insecticide or herbicide. Often there's a toll-free telephone number on the label.

● DON'T smoke, eat or drink when handling toxic or potentially allergenic substances. Change clothes and wash yourself thoroughly after application.

● DON'T mix chemicals; spray only one type at a time. This is especially important when using herbicides.

● DON'T spray on windy days.

● DON'T spray toxic, inorganic insecticides during blossom time or you may kill bees trying to gather pollen.

● DON'T overspray. Apply only the recommended amount and concentration of the product you're using.

HOW PESTICIDES WORK

Contacts kill pests simply by coming in contact with them.

Fumigants are gases which kill when inhaled or otherwise absorbed by the pest.

Pheromones affect pests by changing their behavior.

Poisons kill when swallowed by the pest.

Protectants are applied to plants to keep insects or diseases away.

Systemics are generally absorbed into the plant and transferred to the pest without harming the host.

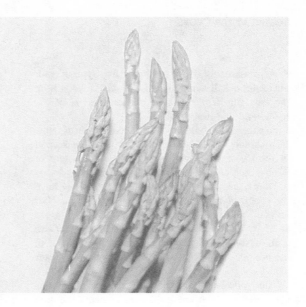

7

Cool Weather Crops

The family of cool weather vegetables, technically known as *Brassica*, is large and varied. The *Brassica* include asparagus, broccoli, Brussels sprouts, cabbage, cauliflower, kale, kohlrabi, lettuce, peas and spinach. They are the first to be planted and the first to emerge in the spring. They can all tolerate freezing temperatures and light snow and have a long growing season. All cool weather crops do best in soil with a pH of 6.0 to 7.0. Peas and kale have a broader range from 6.0 to 8.0.

Asparagus

Asparagus is a perennial that can thrive and be harvested for over 20 years. It often takes three years before the first harvest, however. The root plantings need this much time to develop fully.

The genus *Asparagus* is a member of the lily family originating along the shores of the Mediterranean Sea. The ancient Greeks cultivated asparagus and considered it a delicacy.

Asparagus shoots emerge from an underground root system which can grow up to 10 ft. long. This root system has an extensive network of fleshy storage roots with small feeder roots to absorb water and nutrients. These storage roots are attached to an underground stem called a **rhizome**. The entire root system is commonly called the **crown**. Asparagus shoots develop and rise from the rhizomes and emerge as edible spears.

The asparagus spears you don't harvest develop into an attractive, green, fern-like bush. As this bush matures, it produces carbohydrates and synthesizes other essential nutrients that go to the storage roots. These reserves supply the energy needed to produce spears the next spring. It's important to let these ferns grow so the plant can produce spears next season.

Asparagus can be grown anywhere between the permafrost region of Canada and the extreme southern United States. It does best where the growing season is long and the days sunny for maximum photosynthesis. The ideal daily temperatures during the growing season are from 75°F to 85°F with nighttime temperatures no lower than about 60°F. Asparagus winters well and is not affected by temperatures as low as 40° below zero.

Unlike other vegetables and plants which have both male and female parts on the same plant, the asparagus plant is **dioecious**. The male flowers that produce pollen are on one plant and the female produces berries and seeds. Bees transfer the pollen to seeds. As a rule, male plants have a higher yield and longer life than female plants.

Plant asparagus crowns on a mound inside planting hole. Position root system around and down the mound. Cover with soil.

Asparagus will grow in almost any type of soil, but a little soil enrichment will pay dividends in the long run. The best type will have a pH of 6.0 to 7.0 and will drain well.

Asparagus can be started from seed or from crowns. You should not harvest the spears until the second or third year of growth to give the root system of your crop a chance to establish itself.

Plant asparagus crowns in the spring. If you have the room, plant four to six plants for each member in your family. Cultivate a trench 8 to 10 in. deep and 1 ft. wide. Add compost, 10-10-10 fertilizer and 2 in. of soil. Then plant the crowns on mounds in the bottom of the trench. Cover with soil and water well throughout the season.

The following spring you'll notice asparagus sprouts early. Harvest only a few spears the first year to help build up the reserve food supply in the new root system. The third year should be the beginning of many years of regular harvests.

Today most asparagus strains are seedling populations selected from the Martha and Mary Washington strains developed in the early 1900s. Asparagus breeders in both the United States and Canada are working on new hybrid varieties to offer higher yields and more consistent crops. Some of these new strains include Viking, Glen Smith, California and Jersey selections. Look for seed or root crowns from the major seed companies. Since it can take as long as 30 years to develop a strain of asparagus commercially, it pays to check the seed catalogs every year for new hybrid selections.

Broccoli.

Broccoli

Broccoli is a member of the cole, or cabbage family. Careful timing of broccoli plantings is the key to success. It can be grown in any area that has at least two frost-free months. In areas with short growing seasons, plant in early spring for a summer harvest. If your growing season is longer, you can also plant in the summer for a fall harvest. In regions with very mild winters, late summer and early fall plantings for fall and winter harvests are common. But it should be noted that young plants are hardier than mature plants. Most people agree that fall-harvested broccoli tastes best because the onset of cool weather improves the overall flavor.

Broccoli can be started from seed indoors or planted directly in the garden. The most common approach is to start seeds indoors about 10 weeks before the last frost. After the plants have developed several sets of leaves, they should be hardened off for a week or so in a coldframe before transplanting in your garden. You can move the broccoli plants to the garden three to four weeks before the last spring frost. Cover the plants at night if a hard frost is predicted. Just before transplanting into the garden, strip off the bottom set of leaves. These leaves will probably turn yellow and drop off after transplanting anyway. By stripping them off, they will not sap energy from the plant. A sprinkle of water-soluble transplant solution will help the plant through the initial shock of moving. Space the plants about 10 in. apart.

Summer plantings of broccoli can be made directly in the garden. These will mature in the cool weather of fall. You'll have to allow about 50 to 85 days for a plant to mature after it is transplanted. Allow 65 to 110 days for maturation of seeds after sowing them directly in your garden.

Broccoli seedlings, started indoors, can be planted very early in the garden.

Broccoli will thrive in soil with a pH range of 6.0 to 7.0. Fertile, well-drained, sandy and silt loams are the best types of soils. Work complete garden fertilizer such as 5-10-10 into the soil before you transplant or sow seeds. Good drainage is important for growing broccoli. It can be grown into or through the winter months if your winters aren't too severe.

It's important to harvest broccoli at just the right time for a good tasting crop. Check the center heads of the broccoli often as they develop. Run your thumb over the cluster. As long as the bud remains tightly packed, let the plant grow. When the bud loosens, harvest immediately. If you don't, the bud will produce tiny yellow flowers. This flowering can also be brought on by the onset of hot weather, lack of moisture or stress.

Once you harvest the center and largest bud, many side shoots will form. While these side shoots are smaller than the center bud, they are fine for eating. The small side shoots will also try to flower and must be harvested before this happens.

Some of the more popular varieties of broccoli include Italian Green, Early One, Waltham 29, Green Comet, Green Goliath and Premium Crop Hybrid.

Brussels Sprouts

Brussels sprouts, another member of the cabbage family, do well in cooler weather. Many feel they taste best after a few frosts. This vegetable is a good choice for mid-summer plantings that you can harvest in some regions well into the cooler weather of early winter.

Start seeds for Brussels sprouts indoors 10 weeks before the last frost for an early spring crop. Sow seeds directly in the garden in early to mid summer for a fall crop.

Brussels sprouts tend to be loosely formed and generally of poor quality during warm weather. As cool weather arrives, they tighten up and develop a milder flavor. Encourage the sprouts to form by removing the lower leaves once you see tiny sprouts developing. Harvest the lowest sprouts first as these will be first to mature.

It's a good practice to pinch off the top growth two weeks before first expected frost. This will start sprouts that will all be ready for harvesting at about the same time. If your winters are mild, simply harvest Brussels sprouts from the bottom up until the plant stops producing. Catskill, Jade Cross (F1) and Long Island Improved are popular varieties.

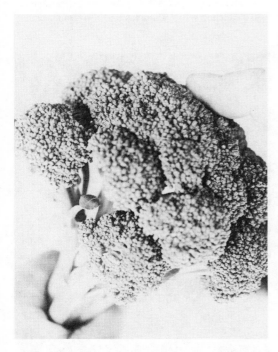

To determine if broccoli head is ready for harvest, rub top with thumb. Bud should be tightly packed and deep green in color.

Brussels sprouts.

Many varieties of cabbages are available for the family garden.

Cabbage

There are several different types of cabbage, among them early, mid and late season, and all have the same requirements for soil conditions and moisture.

Early season cabbages are commonly started indoors 8 to 10 weeks before the last frost. Set plants in a coldframe to harden off for about a week before planting them in the garden. You can harvest early cabbages just as soon as the heads become firm any time during the growing season. These small heads will be less than 6 in. diameter and will weigh from 2 to 4 lbs. Some of the more popular early season cabbages include Early Jersey Wakefield, Primax, Treta, King Cole and Golden Cross. Eat early cabbages right after picking because they don't store well. Use them for coleslaw and other raw or cooked dishes.

Mid-season cabbages can be grown either in the spring or fall. They have medium to large round or flat heads. Start seeds the same way you would for early season varieties for an early crop or in late summer for a fall crop. Harvest mid-season cabbages when the heads are well-filled and hard. They'll weigh from 6 to 12 lbs. This is the most popular variety for making sauerkraut. Red and savoy cabbages are considered mid-season types. The most popular include Copenhagen Market, Enkhuizen, Gourmet, Market Prize and Early Flat Dutch.

Late cabbage is the most common type for storage in a root cellar or other suitable area. This type typically takes over 100 days to mature in the garden. Because of the long growing season, it can be difficult to grow, but it is the best if you are going to store cabbage during the winter. Some of the most popular late cabbage varieties include Green Winter, Safe Keeper, Late Flat Dutch, Burpee's Surehead, and Burpee's Danish Roundhead.

Cauliflower

Cauliflower is another member of the cole family with origins along the Mediterranean Coast. The general soil, pH and water requirements are the same as other *Brassica*.

You can grow cauliflower as a spring or fall crop. For spring, start seeds indoors 6 to 8 weeks before the date of the last frost in your area. After about 4 weeks, place plants outdoors to harden off. Space the plants about 16 in. apart with 24 to 30 in. between rows. Harvest spring cauliflower as soon as the heads reach a suitable size. If you let the cauliflower stay in the garden after it has reached maturity, it will usually go to seed. Harvest it before this happens.

Most of the varieties of cauliflower must be blanched after the head begins to develop. To blanch, simply pull some of the outer leaves over the head. This will keep sunlight from shining directly on it. Blanching keeps the head (sometimes called the **curd**) creamy white and sweet tasting. Some new hybrid varieties of cauliflower do not require blanching.

Many feel the best tasting cauliflower is grown as a fall crop. Start seeds sometime in mid summer and set them into the garden 4 to 6 weeks later. These plants will develop in the fall. Cover the cauliflower heads to protect them if frost is predicted.

The more popular types of cauliflower include Snow King, Snow Crown, Snowflower, Snowball, Self-Blanche, White Empress and Stovepipe.

Cauliflower.

Blanch cauliflower by folding outer leaves over head.

Kale

Kale is a leafy member of the cabbage family that is hearty enough to be overwintered south of Pennsylvania and other areas with similar winter conditions. Soil, pH and water requirements are similar to other members of the cabbage family. Unlike other *Brassica*, kale is very heat resistant and can be grown throughout the summer months. Most gardeners feel the true flavor of kale does not develop until the plant has been lightly frosted.

Kale is commonly grown from seed planted directly in the garden. For a spring and summer crop, plant as soon as you can work the ground early in the spring. For a fall and early winter crop, plant in mid summer.

You can plant kale 8 to 12 in. apart or even closer. With dense plantings, harvest by cutting all the plants off just above the soil line. For wider-spaced plants, harvest only the outer leaves, leaving the bud and a rosette of leaves that will continue growing for later harvests. If kale plants are left in the garden after it freezes, they will start growing when the weather begins to warm the following spring.

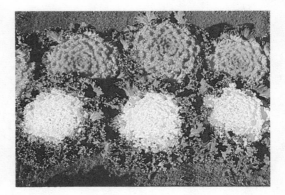

Ornamental kale.

The most popular varieties of kale include Dwarf Blue Curled Vates, Dwarf Siberian, and Dwarf Blue Scotch. You can also grow kale as an ornamental.

Kohlrabi

Kohlrabi, sometimes called an above-ground turnip, is still another member of the cabbage or cole family. It's an interesting vegetable because it's little affected by pests or disease. Kohlrabi is grown under the same conditions as other members of this large family of cole crops.

While kohlrabi can be planted in the spring, most feel that the fall crop yields the best flavor. For your fall crop, plant seeds directly in the garden in mid summer. You'll have to wait an average of 55 to 65 days before you can harvest kohlrabi, and it is tolerant of light frosts. Harvest kohlrabi when the globes are from 2 to 4 inches in diameter and while the flesh is still firm but tender.

Lettuce

It is believed that lettuce originated somewhere in Asia Minor and the Eastern Mediterranean region over 2500 years ago.

Kale.

Kohlrabi.

Head lettuce.

Lettuce is probably the most widely-grown leafy vegetable. A small area in your garden is all you'll need to grow all the lettuce your family can eat. Deep, well-drained soil with an abundance of organic material is best for growing lettuce. The ideal pH is around 6.5 (almost neutral).

Start lettuce seeds indoors 6 to 8 weeks before the last frost. The seeds are tiny and hard to handle. Place lettuce seeds in a salt shaker and sow by shaking them over the soil. Then cover them with about ¼ in. of fine soil. Keep the soil moist during germination. After the plants are about 1½ in. to 2 in. high, move them outdoors to harden off. Put them in the garden as soon after hardening off as possible. Lettuce can tolerate cool weather, but you should cover the plants if a hard freeze is predicted.

Harvest lettuce as soon as the leaves are large enough to eat. Thin by removing leaves or entire plants. Lettuce can be stored for several days in the refrigerator if washed and wrapped in paper towels.

Lettuce is basically a cool weather crop; hot weather will cause most types to bolt and form seed. By making successive plantings throughout the growing season, you should be able to supply plenty for your family. By planting in partial shade, you can often extend the growing season.

Leaf lettuce is easy to grow and tastes great.

The loose-leaf varieties are more widely grown in family gardens than the head types. The most popular loose-leaf varieties include Black Seeded Simpson, Oak Leaf, Green Ice, Ruby, Grand Rapids and Salad Bowl. Head lettuce varieties include Iceberg, Buttercrunch, Bibb, Boston and Parris Island (Romaine).

Peas

Garden peas, often called **green peas** or **English peas**, are the first to be planted in the spring. Peas thrive in cool weather. The best crops will be those that grow rapidly and mature before the onset of hot, mid-summer weather. In areas that do not have hot summers, peas may be grown from spring until heavy fall frosts.

Garden peas are a *legume* and have the unique ability of taking nitrogen directly from the air. They do this with the aid of soilborne bacteria. Because of this, peas don't need a heavy application of fertilizer before planting. A light spreading of 5-10-10 commercial fertilizer a few days before planting is all you need for a bountiful crop.

Use a salt shaker to sow lettuce seeds.

Commercial plant breeder, Dr. N.C. Chen, with his introduction, the Snappy Snap Pea.

Treat seeds with a commercial protectant before planting. Simply moisten the seeds then dust with a powdered legume protectant. This will help keep them from rotting in damp spring soil and give the seeds ready access to needed soil bacteria. You can get legume protectant in garden supply centers and through mail-order seed companies. Occasionally pre-treated pea seeds are available from these same sources.

Depending on the variety, peas can grow anywhere from 18 in. to 6 ft. tall. The lower-growing peas don't generally require support, but the tall vining types must be grown on some type of trellis or netting such as poultry fencing.

Plant pea seeds as soon as you can work the soil in the spring. While most gardening literature and seed catalogs suggest wide spacing between seeds, you can reap large harvests of peas when the seeds are sown as close as an inch apart. Cover the seeds with about 1 in. of fine soil and tamp firmly. As the plants grow, pull about ½ in. of soil around the base of each plant. This will keep the root system moist and cool, resulting in an earlier harvest.

Use two hands to pick peas. Use one hand to hold the vine while the other pulls off the pea pod. One-handed pea picking can damage the vine or uproot the plant.

Harvest peas when the pods are well filled but before they begin to harden or fade in color. Edible podded peas can, of course, be harvested as soon as the pods reach a suitable size. Peas taste best when eaten as soon as possible after picking. The sugar begins to turn to starch when the pea is picked. Freezing the harvested crop can retain the flavor. Pea plants will yield a crop for 7 to 10 days.

Some of the most popular varieties of peas include Little Marvel, Alderman, Wando, Burpeeana Early, Sugar Snap and Snappy.

Broadcast pea seeds for a block planting, then press each seed to the proper depth with your finger, wooden dowel or a spoon.

Protect pea seeds with captan before planting. This will help prevent the seeds from rotting before they germinate.

Spinach

Spinach is a leafy green vegetable that can be grown only in cool weather. For this reason, you'll want to plant spinach seeds directly in the garden as soon as you can work the soil in spring. You can also plant in late summer for a fall harvest. Avoid plantings that will mature during hot weather because plants will bolt—go to seed—rather than produce usable green leaves.

You can grow spinach in most types of soil as long as it drains well and contains an abundance of organic material. The ideal pH range is from 6.0 to 6.8. Work a 10-10-10 fertilizer into the soil before planting seeds.

Plant spinach seeds about ½ in. deep, spacing the seeds about 2 in. apart. As the plants emerge, thin them out, leaving about 6 in. between plants and 18 to 24 in. between rows.

Harvest spinach when there are 5 to 6 leaves per plant. This usually happens about 35 to 45 days after planting. Cut the entire plant off at the soil line. Use spinach fresh in salads, or you can cook or blanch and freeze for later use.

The most popular varieties include Tyee, Blooms-dale Long-Standing, Skookum, and Olympia. Varieties suitable for the far north include New Zealand and cold resistant Savoy.

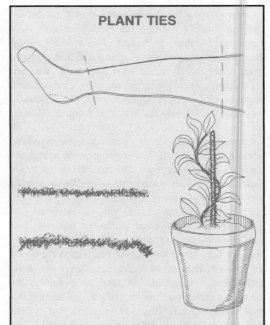

PLANT TIES

Save worn out pantyhose to use as plant tie-backs. After you cut off the tops and bottoms, cut the remaining part into strips about 2 in. wide. Use the strip to tie tall plants to stakes for support. Tie it loosely around the plant and tightly to the stake. The soft, strong nylon material won't cut into the stems. When tomato plants become large, bushy and heavy, you can use a whole "leg" length of pantyhose to tie the branches to the stake or tomato cage. For plant ties that give you even more substantial support and are still soft enough so they won't cut through stems and branches, use your children's old socks. You can also use pipe cleaners for small indoor plants that need support. Push the pipe cleaner into the pot about an inch and wrap it loosely around the stem. The soft covering of the pipe cleaner won't rub or cut the stem.

8

Warm Weather Crops

For many, the warm weather vegetables are what gardening is all about. Included in these crops are beans, corn, cucurbits, eggplant, peppers, New Zealand spinach, Swiss chard and a whole family of herbs. Warm weather crops are well-suited to container growing and are a good choice for urban gardeners.

These crops all require warm soil temperatures. The plants can tell you when it is officially fall, as the first frost will cause at least some of the foliage to turn black and die. Because these crops are grown in the driest months, it's important to water thoroughly. Drought conditions often result in stunted growth or poor yields. There are some steps you can take to keep your summer garden from drying out. Use mulch around the plants to help retain moisture. Weed often to remove competition for moisture and soil nutrients. Harvest vegetables as soon as they reach a usable size; don't let them fully ripen in the garden.

Beans

All beans are members of the *legume* family and all can take nitrogen directly from the air with help from bacteria in the root nodules. Another unique characteristic of this family is the butterfly shape of the flowers. Beans fall into three general categories: snap beans, dry beans and lima beans.

Snap beans are those that are grown for the immature pods and may be called **string, garden, French,** or **green beans**. Since these are not allowed to mature before harvest, their growing season is relatively short making them a good choice for the family garden. Some of the more popular snap beans include Blue Lake, Roma, Kentucky Wonder, and Greensleeves.

Dry beans are similar except that you let the pods develop and partially dry on the vine. Grow dry beans if you want to store them for later use rather than for eating as they're harvested. Dry bean varieties such as pinto, kidney, Great Northern, mung, chickpea and garbanzo are all bush types.

Most vegetables can be grown in containers. Water is important for continued growth.

Bean flowers mean just a few weeks before beans can be harvested.

Kentucky Wonder green beans are one of the most popular varieties.

Lima beans.

Lima beans are grown like other types but generally require a warm, long growing season of 3 to 4 months. Because of this, gardeners in cooler areas don't have much success except with the so-called baby lima types. You eat only the bean after removing it from the large pod.

You can grow beans in a wide range of soils. The best soil is fertile and will drain easily. The ideal pH range is 6.0 to 7.5 for snap and dry beans, 5.5 to 6.5 for lima beans.

With the exception of dry beans, you can get all beans in both bush and pole types. Bush beans produce a usable crop more quickly, but pole beans produce for a longer period of time. Plant bush varieties every 10 to 14 days to be sure of a continuous harvest throughout the growing season. One planting of pole beans should generally supply all your family's needs for a season.

Bush beans are commonly planted in rows 18 to 30 in. apart, with seeds spaced about 1 to 2 inches. After the plants emerge, thin them to about 4 in. apart. Plant all types of bean seeds about 1 in. deep.

Pole beans, because they can reach a height of 8 ft., require some support while growing. This is most easily done with poles, trellises made of post and twine, or with fences.

You'll get about 3 to 4 pickings from bush varieties. Pole varieties seem to yield continuously throughout the season. For both types it's important to pick pole beans at least every other day during the growing period. The overall quality begins to decline after about 3 days, so it's important to keep harvesting as the beans reach a suitable size. Picking beans also encourages the plant to produce pods longer.

Pinto beans.

Pole beans require a support system. These beans bear for an extended period.

Corn

Corn is a native North American cereal that's grown all over the world. It's also known as **maize**. You can get either open-pollinated or hybrid varieties of sweet corn. If your space permits, it's worth experimenting with both types. If you don't have the space, you'll probably have more success with the hybrid varieties.

Sweet corn requires a warm growing season with a minimum soil temperature of about 60°F. While corn will grow in any reasonable garden soil, a clay loam with a pH range of 6.0 to 7.0 seems best. Work a modest application of complete fertilizer (10-10-10 applied at the rate of 5 lbs. per 100 sq. ft.) into the soil before planting.

You can plant corn seeds as early as 3 weeks before the last frost in spring. If you want to harvest sweet corn early, you obviously need to plant it early. Successive plantings, 10 days apart, will guarantee a reliable crop throughout the growing season. Consider early and late maturing varieties. Early types are ready to harvest in about 60 days; late corn is ready for picking in about 90 days.

Because corn seeds are slow to germinate, there is a tendency for the seed to rot in damp, cool soil.

Drench corn seeds in a fungicide like captan before planting to prevent seed rot.

Prevent this by treating with a fungicide protectant before planting. Captan is a good choice.

Plant corn seeds either in 4- to 6-in.-deep furrows or on raised mounds. Furrows are a good choice in dry regions because they help collect water for the plants. Mound plantings are best in wet areas where the hills will shed water and supply just enough moisture for the plant.

Space pairs of seeds about 10 in. apart. Space the rows 18 to 24 in. apart with a minimum of four rows for cross-pollination. Plant the seeds about 1 in. deep. After the plants emerge, thin them out to keep them evenly spaced.

Because corn is pollinated by the wind, you'll need a large enough plot—at least 20 ft. square in most areas—for this to happen.

As corn plants grow, it's often necessary to pile dirt around the base. This helps support the growing plant. Work in 5-10-5 fertilizer around the plants every 3 weeks until silk begins to emerge from the ears.

Corn is ready to harvest when the silk dies and turns dark. To test for maturity, feel the kernels through the husk. If they seem hard and small, the corn is not quite ready to harvest. Check daily. You should never strip back the husk to see if the corn is ready. This is an open invitation to birds and insects.

Cucurbit Crops

Cucurbits are a large family of vining crops that are tropical or semi-tropical in origin. They include cucumbers, gourds, melons, pumpkins, squash and zucchini. All members of this family have similar growing needs; what works for zucchini works for pumpkins.

Another shared characteristic of cucurbits is that they are all capable of taking over a small garden. A pumpkin plant can easily send out a main vine at least 10 ft. long. Two zucchini plants will supply more than enough vegetables to fill the needs of a family of 4 and their neighbors.

Cucurbits will grow throughout the summer months in any well-drained and enriched garden soil. They thrive in soil with large amounts of compost and decomposed animal manure. All cucurbits require a neutral (pH 7.0) or slightly alkaline soil. Soils that are acid—less than 7.0 pH—will result in poor growth and low yield. Test your soil and adjust the pH if necessary for best results.

Cucurbit seeds require a soil temperature of from 60°F to 75°F for germination. Use black plastic mulch to bring your soil temperature up to this range early in the season. Seeds grow best when the outside temperature is from 65°F to 85°F.

Black plastic mulch is ideal for all cucurbits.

Bush cucumbers are a good choice if you have limited space.

The cucurbits are a fairly deep-rooted plant, reaching down to depths of over 3 ft. Because of this, you should supply enough water to maintain a thoroughly moist condition this far down. At least 1 in. of water per week is required, more in arid areas or during dry periods. It's generally better to irrigate the bases of cucurbits rather than shower water from a sprinkler. Moisture on leaves opens the door to foliar diseases which are difficult to control with fungicides.

Plant seeds of cucurbits in hills or mounds of enriched garden soil. Use a rake to form hills with a diameter of about 3 ft. Plant 4 to 6 seeds per hill, 1 to 3 in. deep with equal spacing between each. After the plants emerge, remove all but the best two plants on each hill, ideally on opposite sides of the hill. More than two plants will cause overcrowding and result in poor growth and a low yield. If necessary, you can replant cucurbits in other areas of your garden.

As cucurbits grow, provide ample moisture and fertilizer. A good choice for a complete fertilizer is 5-10-10. Work about ¼ cup of this into the hill before planting seeds. Apply fertilizer again halfway through the growth stage.

Each specific variety of cucurbit has special growing requirements.

Cucumbers. You can grow cucumbers in both vining and bush varieties. If your space is limited, the bush is a better choice. Start seeds indoors or in a coldframe and plant in the garden after all danger of frost. Harvest cucumbers when they reach a suitable size. Small cucumbers are used to make pickles. Remember that large cucumbers are often tough and will contain hard seeds. Picking early lengthens the productive life of the plant.

Popular varieties include Burpee Pickler, West India Gherkin and Chicago Pickling (all for pickles); Bush Champion, Spacemaster, Straight Eight, and Sweet Slice (all for slicing).

Gourds. Gourds are primarily grown for decoration. Many types require a growing season as long as 150 days. Start seeds indoors and transfer to the garden after all danger of frost. If space is limited, train the vines up a trellis or fence. You can halt the growth of these vines by pinching off the ends when they reach a manageable length. Harvest gourds only when fully mature.

Melons. Melons take lots of space in the garden but many feel the space is well invested. Start seeds indoors 3 to 4 weeks before putting the plants out in the garden. Plants should be evenly spaced on hills, 1 or 2 plants per hill. A black plastic mulch over the hill with holes for the plant is a common approach used by gardeners in colder areas. The black plastic helps warm the soil and the melons do better. Growing melons requires adequate moisture with well-drained soil. Watering during drought periods is important. In hot weather, melons may require up to 2 in. water per week.

If you want to grow **cantaloupe**, Burpee's Ambriosia Hybrid and Gold Star are good vine types, and Bush Star Hybrid is a good bush variety. Far North is a particularly hardy variety for colder climates. For **honey dew melons**, look for Venus Hybrid, Limelight Hybrid and Honey Dew. Among the popular **watermelons** are Sweetheart, Burpee's Sugar Bush, Sugar Baby and Triple Sweet Seedless Hybrid.

Pumpkins. Pumpkins are another cucurbit that can take over your garden with a long vine. You can plant pumpkins close to a corn patch, letting the vine snake through the corn rows. They tolerate shade well. Plant seeds in hills after all danger of frost. After plants emerge, thin them out leaving one or two plants per hill. After two or three pumpkins develop, pinch off the end runner and any flowers that develop. This encourages the plant to send all available food to the remaining pumpkins. Fertilize the plant three or four times during the season and water thoroughly. Gently roll the pumpkins every week to prevent flat spots. One-quarter turn is usually enough and will not damage the vine. Harvest pumpkins after the foliage dies but before heavy frost. Cut the pumpkin off the vine, leaving about 6. in. of the stem. Store harvested pumpkins in a cool, dark, well-ventilated place.

Popular pumpkin varieties include Big Max, Triple Treat, Cinderella and Jack-O-Lantern.

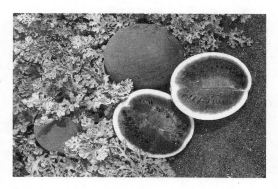

Bush melons are space savers.

Pumpkins are a family favorite.

Summer Squash. Summer squash and zucchini are easy to grow and offer incredible yields. Summer squash does not grow vines. Very little of your garden is used with one of the new space-saving varieties. Plant seeds in hills and thin to one or two plants. Fertilize two or three times during the growing season. Harvest when squash is about 6 in. long for best flavor and texture. For a delicious treat, pick the buds just before the flower opens. Since summer squash continues to produce blossoms you will not appreciably decrease the overall yield.

The more popular varieties of summer squash include Richgreen, Hybrid Zucchini, Pic-n-Pic Hybrid, Butterstick, Burpee's Fordhood Zucchini, White Patty Pan, and Scallop Peter Pan Hybrid.

Winter Squash. You grow winter squash much the same as pumpkins. The benefit of growing winter squash is, of course, that they can be stored and used during the winter months. Let your winter squash grow right up to the first frost. By then the foliage should have died off. Cut the squash from the vine, leaving about 2 in. of vine attached. Any squash without a stem should be used first because it won't last long in storage. Handle the squash carefully to avoid bruising. Cure by letting the skin dry and harden for about 2 weeks. Then store in a cool place (about 50°F) with low humidity. Check stored squash often and remove any that are turning soft.

Popular winter squash varieties include Blue Hubbard, Gold Nugget, Butternut, Acorn, Buttercup, Waltham Butternut, and Table King.

Bush watermelon.

Eggplant

Eggplant, which has been cultivated for hundreds of years, probably had its beginning along the Mediterranean coast. Eggplants fall into four basic categories: round, oval, elongated, and Oriental.

Round eggplants have been available for over 50 years and are probably the most familiar. The most popular are Black Beauty, Beauty Hybrid and Satin Beauty. These develop in 82, 69, and 65 days respectively.

Oval varieties, popular with commercial growers, get to be about 7 in. long and about 3 in. diameter. The most popular varieties for the family garden include Dusky, Black Bell, Epic and Burpee Hybrid. These take between 55 to 70 days before they can be harvested.

Elongated eggplant types, often called **European**, are cylindrical in shape and are not as bulbous as other eggplants. Elongated eggplants are ready to harvest earlier than other types. They reach an average size of 6 to 8 in. long and 2 to 3 in. diameter. Imperial, Blackjack and Baluroi are popular varieties.

Oriental eggplants are the newest introduction by seed companies. They mature quickly (58 days) and do well in cooler climates. Ichiban is the most popular variety. Mature fruits measure about 8 in. long and are about 1½ in. diameter. Tycoon, Millionaire and Money Maker No.2 are also popular.

Growing eggplants. Except for the newer Oriental types, all eggplants need a long and warm growing season. For best results, start the plants indoors 8 to 10 weeks before the last frost. When seedlings have two sets of leaves, transfer them to individual pots and keep them growing under artificial lighting or in a greenhouse. Set plants in the garden after all danger of frost. Often a square of black plastic mulch covering the soil around the plants will help them get the heat they need.

Summer squash.

Winter squash are easy to grow.

Round eggplant.

Oval eggplant.

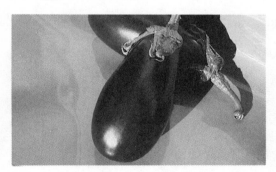

Elongated eggplant.

Oriental eggplant.

Use well-drained and cultivated soil with compost added. The ideal pH range is from 6.0 to 7.0, slightly acid to neutral. Apply a light application of complete fertilizer at planting time and again when the blossoms form. As eggplants grow, it's important to keep the soil moist, especially in hot, dry weather.

Harvest round eggplants when they are about 6 in. long and about 5 in. diameter and the skin is glossy. A dull skin indicates the fruit is past its prime and will contain many hard seeds.

Peppers

The taste range of peppers is probably the widest in the plant kingdom. On one end are sweet green bell peppers that make great snacks. At the other end are the hot varieties; from them we are blessed with such culinary pleasures as Tabasco sauce, salsa and a vast offering of seasoning for ethnic foods. Mexican and Creole foods, for example, both depend highly on hot peppers. There are some peppers that will bring tears to your eyes and sweat to your brow.

Peppers love heat. They do well where days are long and hot. Gardeners in cooler climates often have to plant pepper seedlings covering the soil with black plastic mulch for success.

Another way to succeed with peppers is to choose varieties that generally do well in your area. Local nurseries or garden centers are good sources for these plants. Of course, if you want to try pepper varieties not generally available in your area, you'll have to start from seeds.

When starting pepper seeds indoors, plant them about 8 to 10 weeks before the last frost date for your area. Artificial lighting or a greenhouse are both good aids in growing sturdy plants. Put the peppers in the garden when all danger of frost is past.

The ideal pH for most peppers is from 6.0 to 6.5, slightly acid, with a fairly narrow range. Test and adjust the soil if necessary and work in about one teaspoon of complete (5-10-5) fertilizer per planting. Plant seedlings slightly deeper than they were growing in their pots. Peppers do best when their growth is rapid. Be sure to keep the moisture level around plants constant at all time.

The most popular sweet green pepper is the California Wonder, developed in 1928 in the Los Angeles area. Unfortunately, many areas don't have the same Southern California weather conditions and, as a result, there may be better choices of peppers to grow in your garden. Some other sweet pepper varieties that do well include Ace, Gypsy, New Ace, Canape, and Stokes Early Hybrid. Hot pepper varieties include Zippy, Hungarian Wax, Jalapeno, Cayenne and Big Jim.

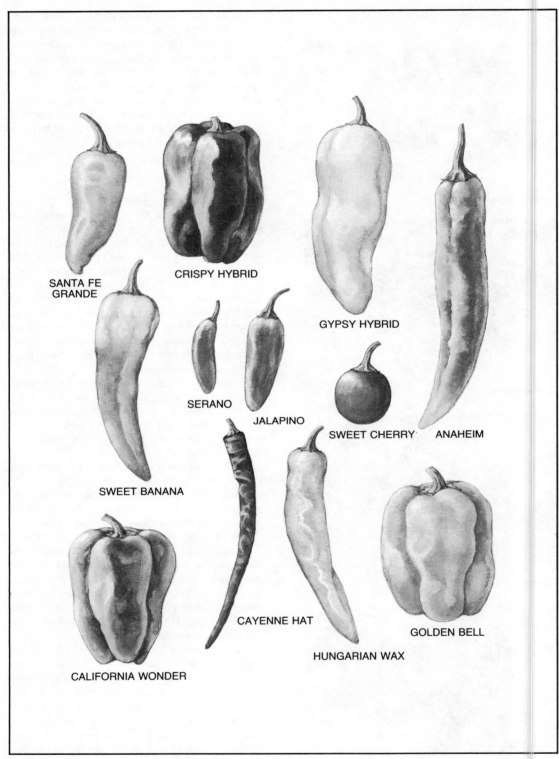

SANTA FE
GRANDE

CRISPY HYBRID

GYPSY HYBRID

SERANO

JALAPINO

SWEET CHERRY   ANAHEIM

SWEET BANANA

CAYENNE HAT

HUNGARIAN WAX

GOLDEN BELL

CALIFORNIA WONDER

It is important to choose varieties of peppers that do
well in your area.

New Zealand Spinach

New Zealand spinach is a native plant of New Zealand, Japan, Australia, and South America. This leafy green vegetable has a taste similar to spinach but because the plant tolerates heat well, you can enjoy it throughout the growing season. True spinach has a limited growing time.

New Zealand spinach requires well-drained, loam soil which is high in organic material such as compost. The ideal pH range is from 6.0 to 6.8. Moisture needs are similar to true spinach. The temperature range which is best for growing New Zealand spinach is from 50°F to 95°F.

Seeds are commonly sown directly into the garden. Work in complete 10-10-10 garden fertilizer before planting. Use about 3 pints per 50-ft. row. Soaking the large seeds for several hours before planting will aid in germination. Space the seeds about 4 in. apart. When plants emerge, thin them to stand about 12 in. apart. Begin harvesting leaves about 70 days after sowing. New Zealand spinach tastes best when cooked rather than eaten raw.

Swiss Chard

Swiss chard grows well in most types of soil that is well-drained. The ideal pH range is 6.0 to 7.0. Apply complete fertilizer, such as 10-10-10, before planting.

Plant seeds about ½ in. deep and about 2 in. apart. Thin them to stand about 12 in. apart during the season. Use the thinned plants as greens or cook them

Herbs

Fresh herbs from the garden add special flavors and over time will save you money. Herbs will grow well in any good garden soil but they also are good for container plantings. They need a minimum of 6 hours of sunlight a day.

Most herbs like a neutral to alkaline soil with pH of 6.5 to 7.5. If you're planning a permanent herb bed, test and adjust the soil before planting.

Herbs may be either annuals or perennials. Annuals are, of course, planted and harvested for one season only. Perennials produce for several years. An herb bed with both types will pay off over time.

You can start herbs from seeds, cuttings or by dividing root stock. Local garden clubs may have sales in early spring offering a variety of small herb plants. Seeds, cuttings and root stock are available from local garden centers, nurseries and larger seed suppliers. Neighbors can also be a good source of herb cuttings and divisions.

Fresh herbs are generally considered better than dried herbs, and their flavor will be much fuller. Dried herbs are, however, a good way of storing them, allowing you to use your herbs until you can grow them again next season.

Some herbs, such as chives, parsley and basil, do well in pots. Before the killing frosts of fall, move the pots indoors to a sunny window sill so you can enjoy fresh herbs during the off season.

Swiss chard.

Basil

Basil is an annual that is commonly started from seed. Plant basil directly in the garden in the spring when the ground is warm and there is no more danger of frost. Basil plants like full sun and moderately rich, moist soil, but they will tolerate semi-shade. They grow to a height of 1 to 2 ft. and can make an attractive border for your garden. Plants produce shiny green leaves and small, white, spikey flowers. To keep the sharp, spicy, clove-like flavor, do not fertilize. Water regularly and frequently pinch the stem tips back so the plants grow bushy and full.

You can use basil in several forms: fresh sprigs either whole or chopped up; dried, either whole or crumbled; frozen, especially if you have chopped it first and added a little olive oil. Another way of preserving basil is curing it with salt. To do this, first wash and rinse the leaves and pat them dry with paper towels. In a quart jar with a lid, alternate layers of leaves with non-iodized table salt. When you have filled the jar, gently press the leaves down and screw the lid on tightly. Store until you are ready to use them. Remember to rinse the leaves before you use them or you will have too much salt for your recipe. With very little effort, you can have a supply of fresh, or almost fresh, basil all year round.

Bay

Bay is a tree that looks like a shrub. It has shiny, leathery leaves which are dark green on top and pale yellowish-green underneath. Bay likes sun or partial shade. It grows to be a tall tree in cooler climates, especially if it is shaded by other trees. Because bay is a tree, you will be more likely to find it with other trees rather than with herbs at the local nursery. Many people successfully plant bay trees in tubs filled with moderately rich soil.

You can pick bay leaves throughout the year, but the flavor is better in cooking if you use crushed dried leaves. To dry leaves, press them between sheets of absorbent paper. You can also put them in a warm oven for about ½ hour or hang them in a cool, dark place. They will keep their natural green color until you are ready to use them.

Bay leaves are strong and spicy. They are especially good in a bouquet garni or in soup or fish stock. Many people also use them in marinades for poultry, meat and fish.

Bay holds an important place in history. In earlier times, bay was used medicinally for its antiseptic value. Also known as laurel, it was used for wreaths to honor poets and heroes. Later it became a popular material for decorative holiday wreaths.

Chives

A hardy perennial and the most delicate member of the onion family. It's a good choice for container growing or as a border plant. Chives will grow in full sun or partial shade in moist, fairly rich soil.

Although chives may grow as high as 24 in., you will probably keep the clumps shorter by snipping them for cooking. They have attractive purple-rose colored flowers that you can cut for use in floral arrangements.

Common chives are green with hollow, round leaves that taste a little like onions. Chinese chives, or garlic chives, have flat, powdery gray leaves with white clover-like flowers growing in clusters above the tips of the leaves. As the name suggests, the leaves have a mild garlic flavor. Both varieties of chives grow in clumps.

In cold climates, chives often go dormant in the winter. You can put small clumps in pots and bring them inside for the winter so you can cook with fresh chives throughout the year. To divide chive clumps, simply split the roots and replant.

The mild, oniony flavor of chives enhances egg dishes, cheese dishes and green salads as well as gravy and soups. You can use the leaves chopped and fresh, or you can dry and freeze them for future use.

Dill

Dill is an annual that grows to 3-4 ft. tall. The dill plant resembles the feathery, light green leaves of fennel, but the plant is generally shorter and smaller with a sharp, slightly bitter taste that is somewhat like caraway.

Start dill seeds in early spring for a summer crop. Plant them in full sun with good, well drained soil. Small, greenish-yellow flowers grow in umbrella-shaped clusters. In the fall, let some of the flowers go to seed and you can establish a permanent dill section in your family herb garden. Don't try to dig up the roots and transplant. You'll find that dill grows quickly and easily from seed.

Dill was formerly used medicinally. In old Norse, "dill" meant "to lull" and people concocted a liquid by cooking the seeds. This brew supposedly helped children go to sleep easily. Now, of course, dill is widely used for flavoring soups, salads, pickles, fish sauces, salad dressings and stews. Both the seeds and the leaves are good seasonings for fish, chicken and lamb. It is also used to make pickles from cucumbers.

You can use dill fresh or dried, but you will derive the *best* flavor from dill which has been picked just as the flowers are opening. You can also use dried dill foliage in flower arrangements.

Marjoram

Marjoram is a tender perennial that can be started from seed indoors 8 to 10 weeks before the last frost. Marjoram can also be grown as an annual or indoors in containers if you live where winters are severe. Marjoram prefers full sun and does best in an alkaline, moist soil. It grows 1 to 3 ft. tall.

The stems of marjoram plants are quite woody and they have small, oval leaves, grayish green underneath and pale green on top. Look for small, pale, almost white flowers that stem from knot-like clusters of tiny leaves growing close together at the tips of the stems.

To grow marjoram, you can sow seeds in the spring, divide the roots or reproduce them from stem cuttings. Make sure you prune the plant periodically and cut off the flowers. If you have enough winter sun on a window sill, bring some of your marjoram plants inside.

Use marjoram as a seasoning for salads, vinegar, casseroles, meats, and as the primary ingredient for marjoram tea and jelly.

There are some interesting folk customs concerning marjoram. It was said that Venus created it, and the sweet smell of the leaves came from her touch. Bridal couples in ancient Greece and Rome wore marjoram wreaths, and bags of marjoram scented people's clothes while they were being stored.

Mint

Mint is a hardy perennial that likes shade. There are many varieties of mint so you can experiment with many different "flavors" and share cuttings with your friends. Mint plants are typically hardy; they grow from 1 to 3 ft.; they like a moist, rich soil; and they differ from most other herbs because they thrive in the shade. The most popular varieties are spearmint and peppermint.

The peppermint plant can grow as tall as 3 ft. It gives off a rich aroma when you touch the leaves. If it starts to go to seed, small purple flowers will grow at the ends of the green stems.

The spearmint plant is another popular variety. If you like eating lamb, you are probably familiar with the mint jelly that comes from this plant. Its dark green leaves are somewhat smaller than the peppermint's leaves.

Mints have played significant roles in Greek mythology and Biblical customs. In the Bible, the pharisees paid their taxes in mint leaves. Later, doctors used mint leaves as an antidote for indigestion, mad dogs and periodontal diseases.

Today, mint is a popular flavor for products that suggest cleanliness. Think of how many toothpastes, mouthwashes, medicines and chewing gums are mint flavored.

CONTROLLING THE SPREAD OF MINT

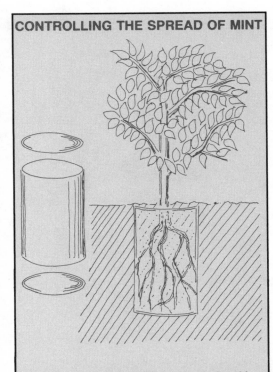

Mint is a wonderful addition to a garden. You can use it for mint sauce, seasoning in salads, garnishes, fruit desserts and gentle flavoring for iced tea. But, it can be a problem in the garden because of the way the roots spread. You can easily keep mint plants from pushing out their roots and robbing nourishment from nearby plants. Cut the top and bottom off a large tin can about the size of a coffee can. Sink it into the ground and work it down all around the plant so the top of the can is even with the soil line. The mint will grow well but the can will keep the roots from spreading too far. If your herb garden is in a window box or planter, you can use smaller cans with the same results.

Oregano

Oregano is a hardy perennial closely related to marjoram. Oregano grows to 2½ ft. in height and prefers full sun and average, well drained soil. You can start oregano from seeds, cuttings, divisions or from plants bought at your local nursery. Oregano has rounded leaves that come to a blunt point at the tip. It has small, purplish pink blossoms. Like mint varieties, it spreads by underground roots.

You need to water oregano routinely and keep the flowers cut back. Because of its height, you'll want to place oregano in the back of your herb garden. You can also grow it in a container. In either case, pick enough of it at the end of the growing season to dry and preserve it for use during the winter.

According to legend, a servant slipped and dropped a large container of the king's favorite perfume. Fearing the worst of the king's wrath, he fainted, and awoke to be transformed into a large, bushy, fragrant plant—the oregano!

The leaves of oregano have a sharper flavor than marjoram and taste somewhat like thyme. Use them as you would marjoram or thyme, especially in Mexican, Italian and Spanish dishes. Harvest the stems and leaves as soon as the flowers appear. Dry the cuttings in small bunches in a cool, dark place.

Parsley

Parsley is a hardy biennial that is tricky to grow from seeds because they might not sprout for up to three weeks. The easiest way to establish parsley is to buy plants. Parsley blooms for two years, but most gardeners treat parsley as an annual for the best yield. Parsley plants like shade or partial sun, and they prefer moist, moderately rich soil. Because they grow to only 6-12 in., they are good border plants.

Although cooks who are most interested in flavor might prefer Italian, or plain-leafed, parsley, most gardeners prefer the curly French parsley which is decorative and almost as tasty. The leaves of French parsley are tufted with wrinkled surfaces and serrated edges.

If your winters are mild, you can sow parsley seeds directly into the soil any time from December to May. Otherwise, sow the seeds in Spring after all danger of frost. Soak the seeds overnight in warm water and plant, remembering that they take a long time to germinate. Thin the seedlings to 6 or 8 in. apart. Harvest the leaves before the plants flower. Once the spikes form, the leaves will be bitter.

In ancient Greek and Roman times, people used garlands of parsley sprigs hung around their necks to absorb alcohol and thus prevent drunkenness!

Rosemary

Rosemary is a hardy, evergreen perennial that requires a well drained, slightly alkaline soil and plenty of direct sunlight. It will survive even in poor soil, and except for extremely hot climates, established rosemary plants require little watering. If you live where winters are mild enough, rosemary creates an excellent perennial shrub.

Rosemary leaves are narrow and look like pine needles. They are a grayish green color underneath and are a darker, shinier green on top. They smell like pine needles, and they produce pale lavender-blue clusters of flowers.

There are some interesting legendary references to rosemary. The Virgin Mary is said to have given the bluish-lavender color to the rosemary flowers when she placed her blue cape to dry on a rosemary bush. Rosemary also figured in early rituals, being carried at weddings and placed on coffins after funerals. Rosemary was also supposed to improve memory and prevent nightmares!

Today, rosemary is an especially good accompaniment to chicken and lamb, and it is tasty in stews and vegetable dishes. Next time you cook chicken on the grill, use a branch of rosemary as your barbecue brush. You can also use rosemary leaves to make an aromatic tea.

DRYING HERBS

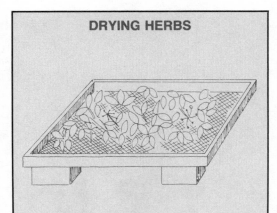

Many of the herbs you grow can be dried to use later. Remove heavy stems, then lay the greens on a piece of window screen or a coarse sieve. Thin layers of herbs dry more quickly. Put the screen in a dark, dry place, propped up on a couple of pieces of wood to let the air move freely all around. Test leaves every few days until they crumble when you touch them. Then push the herbs through the screening and pack the finely sifted herb in a small jar with a lid that closes tightly. You can also hang the herbs upside down to dry in the basement. If you have a dark space with wooden beams or unfinished wall space where you can staple directly, the single stems get plenty of air circulation and dry hanging out of your way. Do the same with stems of wild flowers. Once dried, they add natural beauty to fall arrangements and you can just throw them away later, knowing how easy it will be to dry some more next year.

Sage

Sage is a hardy evergreen perennial that can be started from seed or nursery stock. Sage grows to 2 to 3 ft. in height and prefers full sun and poor, dry, well drained soil. Water from the ground rather from the top of the plant and avoid overwatering. Prune the stems after the flowers bloom, and fertilize periodically. Sage deteriorates quickly and should be raised from cuttings at least every four years.

Garden sage is the most common variety. It grows to about 2 ft. tall and has grayish-green leaves shaped like elongated ovals. The leaves have a coarse surface and feel bumpy. Garden sage has a lavender-blue flowers on tall spikes. Long ago, garden sage was highly valued for its medicinal qualities and people thought it would help with such problems as stomach disorders, broken bones and memory loss.

Two other popular varieties of sage are the pineapple sage and the clary sage. The pineapple sage has scarlet flowers in the fall and produces a delightful fragrance from its green leaves. Clary sage has large leaves that taper to small leaves at the top of the plant.

To make sage tea, take a handful of the leaves, the juice and rind of one lemon and a teaspoon of sugar and steep for for several minutes.

Tarragon

Tarragon is a perennial which must be started from cuttings or root division. It has a shallow root system which must be protected from extremely cold weather. Tarragon spreads slowly by its creeping rhizomes. It has shiny, dark green leaves that are slender at the top. Unlike may other herbs, its flowers are very small and seldom seen.

Tarragon grows to 1-2 ft. in height and prefers moderately rich, well drained soil. Gardeners like to plant tarragon because it does not require full sun; in fact, it does best in a warm place with partial shade. The leaves of the tarragon plant have a strong, distinctive flavor somewhat like licorice or anise. The name itself seems to come from the strong flavor of the leaves. In French, "estragon" means "little dragon."

Most other herbs should be harvested for drying just before they have flower buds, but you should harvest tarragon for drying during August. If you're going to use it for vinegar, harvest it in July. In this case, gather the tarragon, pick the leaves off the stalks and put them in a bottle—8 oz. of leaves to every 2 qts. of vinegar.

Tarragon is good for fish, egg and cheese dishes, and in salads.

Thyme

Thyme is a hardy perennial that can be started from seed, root divisions or nursery stock. Select a sunny location for thyme and plant it in dry, light soil. The plants do not need much attention, and you should be careful not to overwater them. They are low, bushy plants with attractive blooms. There are many varieties of thyme and they are used as ground covers, as herbs for their aroma and flavor, and as ornamentals.

The most widely used for cooking is the common thyme. This is a relatively short shrub, growing to only 6½ in. high and spreading out as much as 1½ ft. It has small flowers that grow at the end of the spiked stems, and it has grayish-green leaves that form ovals about ¼ in. long.

You might want to find other varieties of thyme at your local nursery: mother-of-thyme is useful as a filler for small areas in the garden; silver thyme has small leaves, variegated with silver; lemon thyme has a delightful aroma and is variegated with yellow; wooly thyme is another good ground cover; and caraway-scented thyme forms a matted ground cover and smells like caraway.

Historically, thyme has been associated with happiness, health and courage.

9

Root Crops

The family of root crops is large and you'll probably want to try several different varieties in your family garden. Some of the varieties of root crops include beets, carrots, garlic, horseradish, Jerusalem artichoke, leeks, onions, parsnips, potatoes, radishes, rutabaga, shallots and turnips.

You can start root crops in the spring as soon as you can work the soil. Since root crops love cool weather, they are not damaged by light frosts. In fact, many gardeners feel the overall flavor improves with the onset of cool weather. Carrots, for example, taste better when pulled late in the fall rather than in the summer.

You can enjoy root crops long after the growing season. They store well in dark, cool areas—that's how root cellars got their name.

Sow these seeds heavily and thin the plants as they emerge, taking out the largest first. This will allow the other plants to develop quickly.

Beets

Table beets grow best in cooler weather. Because of this, they are generally grown late in the season for harvest after the fall frost for storage. They can also be grown early in the season, as soon as the ground can be worked, for summer eating. There are also varieties available for the far northern areas that are smaller and mature more quickly than the standard types.

Beets grow best in well-drained soil that crumbles easily and is adequately supplied with fine organic materials. Cultivate to a depth of about 9 inches. Raised beds with these soil conditions are ideal for growing beets. The ideal pH range for all beets is from 6.2 to 7.0, almost neutral.

There are two basic types of beets: table beets and sugar beets. Table beets are, as their name suggests, used for eating. Sugar beets, on the other hand, are a commercial cousin of the table beets. They are grown primarily for processing into white sugar. The ideal table beet will often be a hybrid between the table and sugar beets. The hybrid Big Red, for example, has an 18% sugar content.

Beets.

Good growth for table beets depends not only on good soil conditions but also on a supply of nitrogen. Before planting seeds, sprinkle bone meal or superphosphate fertilizer (such as 0-20-0) over the seedbed at a rate of about 1 cup per 10 sq. ft. An application of 5-10-10 fertilizer while working the soil before planting will eliminate the need to fertilize during the growth stages. Phosphorus encourages fast and constant root growth, so adding bone meal before planting will ensure that plenty of this mineral will be available to the plants.

Hybrid beets will mature from 10 to 14 days earlier than open-pollinated varieties. The most popular open-pollinated beets include Detroit Dark Red, Early Wonder and Ruby Queen. The most popular hybrid beets include Red Ace and Pace Maker III.

You might want to sow beet seeds heavily. Many people find that about a third of the seeds never seem to germinate. A row about 3 ft. long is all you'll need for the initial planting. As the seeds emerge, thin slightly until seedlings are about 1½ in. high. You can then dig up the row and transplant the seedlings into a raised bed where they can be harvested as they grow. Space the seedlings about 3 in. apart.

You can also sow seeds heavily in seed flats and then transplant into the garden when the seedlings are about 1 to 1½ in. high.

Choose carrot varieties that will do well in the soil type of your garden.

Carrots

Carrots will grow in almost any type of soil as long as it is moist, fertile, loose and free from clods or stones larger than an inch. Sandy loam and peat soils are best. Cultivate the soil at least 8 in. deep. Carrots will thrive in soil with a pH from 5.5 to 6.5. It's important to adjust your soil pH before planting.

Often the difference between success and failure lies in choosing the right variety of carrot. Long, slender commercial types are difficult to grow in the family garden. Instead, choose varieties that grow to a maximum length of only 5 or 6 inches. The taste of these shorter varieties is just as good—sometimes better. Some of the most popular shorter length carrots include Nantes Half Long, Royal Chantenay, Goldinhart, and Short 'n Sweet.

For a steady crop throughout the season, make successive plantings about three weeks apart, starting as soon as you can work the soil in the spring. It's far better to sow seed lightly rather than heavily because the growing plants need at least 1 in. spacing. This helps carrots grow to full size without crowding.

Probably the most common complaint among carrot growers is that the roots are misshapen or forked. This can be often be directly attributed to overcrowding. Avoid this by thinning the plants to a 1-in. spacing as soon as they emerge. Other causes for this problem include compacted soil, too much water, heavy fertilization and disease. The shorter varieties are less prone to these problems than are the long, tapered carrots.

Garlic

Garlic is easy to grow and well worth the effort. While it does best when planted in the fall, it can also be planted in early spring for harvesting around the end of the season. Garlic grows well in almost any soil with a pH range of 5.0 to 7.0.

For early spring planting, separate a garlic bulb into cloves and plant them about 4 to 5 in. apart. Push the cloves into the soil until just the pointed tip is exposed. In the fall, these cloves will have matured into garlic bulbs. Harvest when the stems lose all trace of green and the tops bend over to the ground. Pull the bulbs and let them air-dry for a few days before storing. Braid the tops into an attractive and functional rope.

When you plant garlic cloves in the fall, you can expect to harvest large bulbs the following summer. Choose a well-drained, sunny spot and plant individual cloves about 2 in. below the surface. These cloves will sprout early in the spring and yield a crop of large bulbs sometime in late summer.

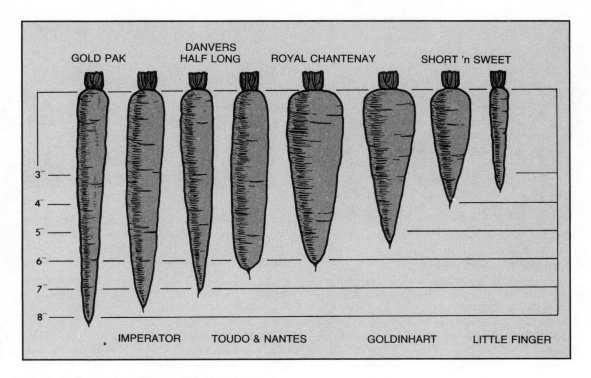

GOLD PAK DANVERS HALF LONG ROYAL CHANTENAY SHORT 'n SWEET

3"
4"
5"
6"
7"
8"

IMPERATOR TOUDO & NANTES GOLDINHART LITTLE FINGER

Garlic bulb must be separated into cloves before planting. Each clove will yield a bulb at the end of the growing season.

Horseradish

Horseradish does best in cooler climates. It's a perennial root used to add zest to a variety of meat and seafood dishes. The mature roots are pulled, cleaned and shredded into horseradish sauce. While you can pull the roots at any time, they are generally best in the spring.

Grow horseradish in deep, rich, well-drained soil that has a substantial amount of organic material. The pH range for horseradish is from 6.0 to 8.0. Plant your horseradish in a location with full sun. Since this is a root crop, remove rocks and other debris from the soil before planting. In preparing the horseradish bed, mix organic material into the soil several months before planting.

Horseradish root cuttings are available from most of the seed companies or get yours from a neighbor with an established patch. New Bohemian is the most popular type for root cuttings.

Till or spade the area about 8 in. deep, mixing in a handful of commercial fertilizer or a generous amount of compost. Push the root cuttings into the bed at a 45° angle and about 2 in. below the surface. Plants from these root cuttings usually make good-sized roots the first season. Pieces of roots and crowns remaining after harvest are usually enough to reestablish a crop for the next season.

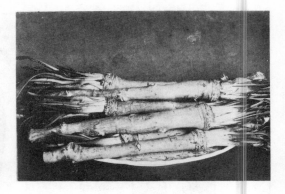

Plant horseradish roots at a 45° angle to the soil line.

Jerusalem Artichokes

Like horseradish, Jerusalem artichokes will grow for years with little attention other than soil conditioning and fertilizing. If left to themselves, Jerusalem artichokes will spread throughout your garden, so it's best to harvest these prolific underground tubers annually.

Plant tubers in an isolated, sunny location. Since the plants can easily grow to 6 ft. high, don't put them where they will shade smaller plants. Cultivate about 8 in. deep, adding organic material or commercial fertilizer. Plant the tubers about 4 in. deep and about 2 ft. apart. Dig the tubers in the fall with a spading fork and store in a cool, dark place. It's time to harvest Jerusalem artichokes when the foliage turns brown and dies. If the ground does not freeze hard in your area, you can store these tubers right in the soil and dig them up as you need them during the winter months. To do this, pile mulch such as leaves or hay on top of the area to protect the ground from freezing hard.

Leeks

The leek looks like an onion but it has a milder flavor. The leek differs from an onion because it produces a thick, fleshy cylinder rather than a bulb. Use leeks and onions interchangeably in cooking.

Leek seeds are commonly started indoors along with onion seeds and planted in the garden as sets. Start seeds 8 to 10 weeks before outdoor planting time. For a later crop you can start leek seeds directly in the garden in the early spring. Space the plants about 6 in. apart in rows 2 ft. apart.

You must blanch leeks to develop the white cylinders. This is simply a matter of pulling soil around the plants up to the base of the green leaves as they grow. This will not only help make the leeks white; it also helps make them tender and better tasting.

You can harvest leeks in the fall when they have developed a cylinder about 1½ to 2 in. diameter. If you can protect your soil from freezing hard, you can also cover leeks with mulch for harvesting fresh during the winter months.

Jerusalem artichoke.

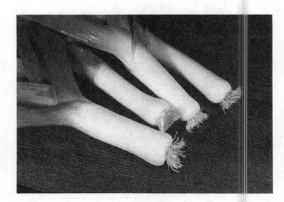

Leeks.

Onions

Since onions grow almost anywhere, they are a good choice for the family garden. You can grow onions from seed, seedlings or onion sets. Of these, the seeds are least expensive but require the most work. Onion plants and sets are more expensive than seeds but are probably the most dependable and the easiest to grow.

Start the seeds indoors in the spring, 8 to 10 weeks before the last heavy frost in your area. The best environment is under grow lights turned on 12 to 18 hours a day. Keep the lights about 4 to 8 in. above the tops of the plants, moving the light up as they grow. Transplant into the garden when plants are about the thickness of a pencil. Space the plants about 2 or 3 in. apart in rows 12 to 18 in. apart.

You can also sow seeds directly into the garden as soon as you can work the soil in the spring. It's important to keep the ground moist during germination. Onions do best in reasonably fertile, well-

important that you harvest these onions with dead foliage as soon as possible. Pull the onions and leave them on the ground with the bottoms upward. If the weather isn't dry, move the onions into a protected area. After a few days of drying, they will be ready for curing—the last step before you store them.

To cure onions, place them in a warm, airy place in the shade. You can cover them with any type of porous material such as burlap or an old bed sheet. Never use plastic. Turn the onions every few days to encourage even curing. After about two weeks, the onions are ready to store. Put them in mesh bags and hang them in your garage or other airy place where they can cure for another two weeks. Almost any shaded area that does not freeze is okay. Finally, after about two weeks in the mesh bags, transfer the cured onions to any dry, cool place for storage. It's important to check them often and remove any that are not cured properly or those that are beginning to rot.

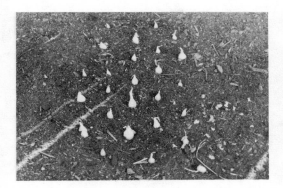

Plant onion sets for faster growth than seeds.

drained, well-prepared soil with an abundance of organic matter; but without stones or other debris.

If you're using onion plants or sets, put them out in the garden as soon as you can work the ground in the spring. Both onion seedlings and sets should be planted in furrows about an inch deep. Lightly press the sets or the base of the seedlings and cover with soil. Space plants about 3 in. apart in rows about 18 in. apart.

Onions need ample organic matter and fertilizer during growth. Use a good general fertilizer such as 5-10-10 before planting. During the growth stage, side-dress the plants with bone meal.

As onions grow from seeds, plants or sets, you should thin occasionally to prevent crowding. You can use these thinnings as scallions. In the fall, the green leaves will lose their color and wither. It's

Parsnips

Mature parsnips look like large white carrots. They have a unique sweet flavor. If you plant them in the spring, they are ready to harvest in late fall. You can also leave them in the soil through the winter and harvest in the early spring. Many gardeners feel that parsnips taste better after they have been frozen.

Parsnip seeds are slow to germinate. In fact, they may not sprout at all if they are more than a year old. Sow seeds heavily then thin the plants to stand about 4 to 6 in. apart. It can take as long as 2 weeks for parsnips to sprout, so be patient.

As with many other root crops, parsnips grow best in deeply-cultivated soil that has an abundance of organic material. Before planting seeds, till or spade the soil about 8 to 12 in. deep, removing any rocks or other debris that might cause the roots to become misshapen. Work in a complete garden fertilizer such as 5-10-5. After planting, water well.

Potatoes

White potatoes are one of the most productive of all vegetables in terms of amount of food per unit of garden space. Potatoes are a cool-season crop; they don't thrive in the heat of mid summer or in very hot regions.

Potatoes grow from the "eyes" of the potatoes themselves. Certified seed potatoes are best and some of the more popular types include Kennebec, White Cobbler, Red Pontiac, and Red Norland. There is also Keswick or Norgold Russet for the far northern regions.

Small seed potatoes (golf-ball size) can be planted without cutting. Cut large potatoes into sections that contain 2 or 3 eyes or buds and let them air-dry a few days to harden off the exposed surface. Treat the freshly cut chunks with sulfur power as an inexpensive, natural protectant. The sulfur will also lower the general pH around the growing seed—potatoes thrive in a lower pH soil.

cause the skin to turn green and produce a toxic rather than an edible skin. Avoid eating any potato with a green skin. Hilling is most easily done by pulling soil around the base of the plant with a hoe. Hill the plants when they are about 3 to 5 in., then again when they are about 8 to 10 in. high.

Harvest some of the potatoes after about 2 months of growing. The potatoes then will be small but quite tasty. Simply dig down with a spading fork and lift out a few small potatoes from around each plant. These early potatoes are a real garden treat.

Once the potato foliage begins to wither and die, it's time to start harvesting for storage. Dig up the potatoes with a spading fork. Dig around the plants about 18 to 24 in. down from the base of the plant. Be careful not to pierce the potatoes with the fork. If you do, use these first. Let harvested potatoes air-dry before storage. Just let the potatoes lie on the surface for a few days to harden off the skins. If rain is predicted, move them to a covered, airy

Potato.

Potatoes that have been cut must be protected with agricultural sulfur before sprouting to prevent rot and to help lower the pH in the soil, creating a slightly acid condition which potatoes like best.

The ideal pH range for white potatoes is from 4.8 to 5.5, slightly acid. The area you plan to use for potatoes should not be manured the previous season as this will generally increase the pH to over 6.0. Potato scab, a fungus disease on the surface skin, tends to be quite active in the 6.0 pH range. While this disease does not ruin the tubers, it does disfigure the skins.

There are several ways to cultivate potatoes. The most common is planting in furrows, cultivated 6 to 8 in. deep. Using this method, till a trench and sprinkle the bottom with 5-10-10 fertilizer. Next, put a 3-in. layer of soil over the fertilizer. Then put the seed potatoes in the row, cut side down, and cover with at least 4 in. of soil.

As your potatoes grow, they must be hilled so the tubers will not be exposed to the sun. This would

spot. After a few days of drying, store in a cool, dry area such as a garage, basement or a root cellar if you have one.

You can also grow potatoes using the mulch method. While this will not generally yield as many potatoes per plant as the trench method, it requires almost no work. Seed potatoes are simply placed on the ground and covered with 1½ to 2 ft. of hay mulch. All that's required until harvest is to keep the mulch watered regularly.

Harvesting mulch-grown potatoes is simple. Just brush the mulch aside and gather the potatoes. Harden off the skins of mulch-grown potatoes the same way you would the trench crop.

Plant cut potato halves, each containing at least two eyes or buds, in a thick layer of straw. As plants grow, add more straw to keep covered. To harvest, simply brush aside the straw and pick the tubers.

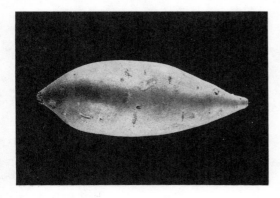

Sweet Potatoes

Most varieties of sweet potato grow best in regions where there are at least 150 frost-free days during the growing season. For this reason, sweet potatoes are grown commercially throughout the southern part of the United States. There are, however, new varieties available that will mature in 100 days. Sweet potatoes can, therefore, be grown farther north if they are started indoors about 8 weeks before the average last frost date—anywhere, that is, with at least 50 to 100 frost free days.

Grow sweet potatoes from slips. These are tiny plants sprouted from the sweet potato. You can get these from your local supermarket or from seed companies. The more popular varieties include Jersey Orange, Nuget and Nemagold for warmer climates; Centennial, Puerto Rico and Gold Rush for cooler regions.

Sweet potatoes grow best in soil that is slightly acid, 5.0 to 6.0 pH. A well-drained, moderately deep sandy loam of medium fertility is best. Very deep, loose-textured soils encourage long stringy roots. For best results, you should fertilize the soil moderately. If you apply garden fertilizer directly to the row, mix it well with the soil.

Once established, sweet potatoes are drought-hardy and will produce a fair crop even under very dry conditions. By supplying ample moisture, however, you'll generally increase the overall yield of tubers. The plants require about ¾ in. of water per week when small and up to 2 in. of water during vigorous growth in hot weather. Excessive moisture may cause the sweet potatoes to crack, but this will not generally affect eating or storing quality.

Sweet potatoes do not ripen or mature, so decide when to harvest them by their root size. 110 to 120 days after transplanting (sooner for quicker growing varieties), check the size of the roots. Dig carefully around one or more plants. If the tubers have reached the size you want, harvest them. A light frost will damage the foliage but does not affect the quality of the potato.

After you dig sweet potatoes, you must cure the roots before storing them. Put the potatoes in an area where the temperature is about 85°F with a relative humidity of 85% to 90% for 6 days. You can create this high humidity by wrapping the potatoes loosely in plastic bags. Don't cure in the sun because sweet potatoes sunburn easily.

After they're cured, store the roots in a cool place (55°F to 60°F) with a high relative humidity. An unheated area of your basement or garage is generally suitable.

Radishes

Radishes are the quickest of all vegetables to grow in the family garden. That's why they're a good project for children. Radishes can withstand cold weather, but they cannot withstand extreme heat at all. In regions where summers are very hot, grow radishes in the spring and fall. Elsewhere they may be grown throughout the season. In regions having a very mild winter, you can grow radishes in cold-frames.

White radish.

You can grow radishes in almost any type of soil as long as it is rich, moist and loose. The ideal pH range is from 6.0 to 8.0, slightly alkaline. The best tasting radishes are those that grow quickly; those that grow slowly have an unpleasant flavor and woody texture. Since radishes remain in prime condition for only a few days, it's important to harvest them as soon as possible. By making successive plantings of seeds every ten days you'll have all the radishes you and your family can possibly eat.

Because they are so quick to sprout and grow, radishes are handy for companion planting with other vegetables that are slow growers. By planting a few with parsley, carrots and parsnips, the radish plants will let you know where the rows are. By the time you harvest them, the other vegetable in the row will be well on its way.

There are two basic types of radishes. The first is small, mild and quick growing, such as Scarlet Globe, French Breakfast and Cherry Belle. These reach picking size in 20 to 40 days. The second type is called a winter radish. It requires 70 or more days to mature. Some of the most popular of this type include Long Black Spanish and China Rose. Store winter radishes like other root crops such as carrots, beets and potatoes.

Rutabagas and Turnips

Rutabagas and turnips are similar cool-season vegetables. Rutabagas do best in the cooler regions, while turnips are a better choice for gardens in the south. Turnips reach a good table size in 60 to 80 days; rutabagas mature about a month later.

Although there are both white and yellow turnips and rutabagas, most turnips are white and most rutabagas are yellow. Purple Top White Globe and Just Right are the most popular white varieties of turnip; Golden Ball is the most popular yellow turnip. American Purple Top is a commonly grown yellow rutabaga; Sweet German, White Swede and Sweet Russian are the most widely used white varieties.

Soil with a pH range of 6.0 to 8.0 is best for these root crops. Plant seeds as soon as you can work your garden in the spring. The soil need not be prepared deeply, but the surface should be fine-textured and smooth. Row planting gives the best results.

Shallots

Shallots, like onions, belong to the lily family. Shallots have bulbs less than 2 in. long and 1 in. diameter. The leaves are hollow and small and can also be used like chives.

Shallots are planted in the early spring along with onions, garlic and other cool weather crops. For the largest bulbs, in mild regions, plant in the fall and harvest the next year. They grow best in light, loose and well-drained soil. The ideal pH range is 5.0 to 7.0. Garden soil should have abundant amounts of organic material such as compost or peat moss for heavy yields.

Shallots are very productive. One pound of seeds yields about five to seven pounds of shallots. Let the sets grow until the foliage begins to die back. Then pull the bulbs, air dry in a shady location for several days and keep in a cool, dark place. Shallots keep longer than other root crops, up to 12 months under ideal conditions.

10

Tomatoes

Growing tomatoes is popular among family gardeners. Tomatoes have a unique flavor, they're attractive, rich as a source of vitamins C and A, and are versatile as a food. They are easy to grow and easily preserved by canning, freezing or drying.

The cultivated tomato originated in the Andes mountains of South America. It was introduced to the rest of the world by European explorers and travelers. Tomatoes were first grown in North America around 1710, primarily as an ornamental plant. It was not until around 1820 that tomatoes began to gain acceptance as a food crop.

The average person consumes around 50 lbs. of tomato-related products each year. There is a vast agricultural industry for such products as ketchup, tomato sauce and canned tomatoes.

Many of the attractive, round, red tomatoes at the local supermarket have almost no taste at all. The reason for this is really one of economics for tomato growers. Tasty tomatoes don't travel well and have a short shelf life. Tomato growers have developed new varieties that have many desirable marketing characteristics but, unfortunately, little taste when compared with home grown tomatoes.

SELECTING TOMATOES

You are not restricted to only a few types in your choice of which tomatoes to grow. In fact, a quick glance through any seed catalog will show at least 20 different varieties for the family garden. Try growing several different types to discover which grow best in your area of the country. Keep in mind that some are early blooming and bear fruit only once while others may bear tomatoes up until the first frost.

Types of Tomatoes

Some of the more popular early types of tomatoes include Burpee's Early Girl, Gurney's Cold-Set, and Spring Set VF. For the more "standard" garden tomatoes the popular types include Super Beefsteak VFN, Rutgers, Roma VF, Burpee's Big Girl Hybrid VF, Burpee's Supersteak Hybrid VFN and Campbell's 1327 VF. If you're considering growing tomatoes in containers, good choices are Burpee's Pixie Hybrid, Basket King Hybrid and Tiny Tim.

All tomatoes are either "determinate" or "indeterminate," terms which indicate the type of growth and harvest you can expect from the plant. It makes good sense to grow both types to have fresh tomatoes all season long.

Determinate varieties set and ripen all their fruits at nearly the same time. They have a terminal leader or main stem that develops a flower bud at the top of its growth. These are good choices for home canning when you want a lot of tomatoes at about the same time.

Indeterminate tomato varieties continue to grow and set fruit the entire growing season. They are a good choice for trellising, staking or caging. The main stem does not develop a flower and allows continued growth.

Disease Resistant Types

When looking through catalogs for tomato seeds, you'll often see the letters VF or VFN after the name.

V indicates resistance to verticillium wilt.

F indicates resistance to fusarium wilt.

N indicates resistance to nematodes.

The wilt diseases and nematodes live in the soil for many years. The only way to avoid the problems they can cause is to choose seeds with VF or VFN designations.

Start tomato seeds six to eight weeks before setting out in the garden. These healthy plants are ready for planting.

STARTING TOMATOES FROM SEEDS

Tomatoes are highly sensitive to cold. The farther north you live, the less luck you'll have and the more work growing tomatoes will be. At least part of the success for growing tomatoes from scratch is to start the seeds indoors six to ten weeks before the last frost date for your area. After that date you can set the plants out in the garden.

Equipment Needed

Starting tomato seeds indoors is easy, but some specialized equipment will increase your chances of success. You will need some type of artificial lighting for optimum growth. A 4-tube fluorescent light fixture which you can raise or lower above the growing plants is probably the most effective and least expensive system for indoor seed sprouting.

Before you start tomato plants indoors you'll need to gather a selection of seeds, planting mix and containers. Make sure you have a warm place to germinate and grow the plants.

Soil for Seeds

While you can buy commercial planting mixes, you can also mix up your own. Combine equal amounts of peat moss, perlite or vermiculite and sand. This mixture is an ideal growing medium for any small plant because it doesn't compact, and strong root systems develop easily.

Seeds can be started in almost any type of container, but you'll find that the plants are easier to manage if all containers are about the same size and shape. It's important that the containers have holes in the bottom or sides so excess water can drain. Some people prefer small peat pots or 2-in. plastic pots. Others have success with empty egg cartons.

Planting the Seeds

Begin by moistening the planting mix and fill the containers almost to the top. Sprinkle about 3 to 4 tomato seeds in each container, spaced about ¼ to ½ in. apart. Firm the seeds into the mix with a spoon or a flat piece of wood, then cover them with about ¼ in. of fine moist soil. Firm the soil over the seeds so they are in direct contact with the moist planting mix. This will encourage germination. The last thing to do is to cover the pots with plastic. A large plastic bag works well, especially if your containers are in a nursery tray. Covering with plastic helps retain as much moisture as possible. The plastic bag acts like a miniature greenhouse for the first few days. When the tomato plants sprout, remove the plastic.

Under ideal conditions of heat and moisture, tomato seeds will sprout in 3 to 5 days. It's important that you keep the temperature a constant 65°F to

70°F during germination. Some good places to put the seed containers to sprout would be on top of your refrigerator or on top of a water heater or furnace. A window sill is generally **not** a good place because there is always a drop in temperature after the sun goes down.

Once the seeds have sprouted, remove the plastic and put the plants in a sunny window or under a fluorescent fixture. If you put the plants on a window sill during the day, you'll have to move them to a warmer spot during the night. The cool air around the window will inhibit growth.

Grow lights

A fluorescent light fixture is good to use when you grow plants indoors. Look in your garden center or hardware store for fluorescent tubes especially designed for growing plants. At first, put the new seedlings about 2 in. below the lights.

Try to maintain this distance between the plants and grow light throughout the time the plants are under the lights, raising the light fixture as the plants grow. If you place the plants much farther away than 2 in. they will stretch for the light and become spindly and thin.

When growing tomato seedlings under fluorescent lights, it's important to remember that plants require both light and dark. Turn the lights off for 8 hours every 24-hour period. An automatic timer is a reliable and worthwhile part of your indoor growing system.

Caring for the New Seedlings

As the tomato plants grow, you must water them daily. Keep the soil moist, not wet. There are several schools of thought about watering seedlings, but tomatoes should grow well if you use water at room temperature and mist spray the plants rather than pour water on them. Watch for signs of damping off (too much moisture) or of drying out.

After a few weeks, it'll be time to thin out tomato seedlings. Keep only one or two of the strongest plants per pot.

When a second set of leaves develops and the plants are about 3 to 4 in. tall, it will be time to put them in larger containers. Put only one plant in each pot. Water the seedlings well before transferring them. Transplant them deeply to encourage stronger root systems. When the stem of a tomato plant is buried, roots will develop from it. The result is always a strong root system. Water the plants with a water-soluble fertilizer once a week.

As the seedlings grow you may notice some problems such as legginess, spindliness, or stunted growth. Almost always these problems can be directly attributed to poor lighting, overwatering, overfertiliz-

ing or drafty conditions. Often the best cure is to replant the seedling in a larger pot with fresh soil. Take off all but the two top sets of leaves and bury the plant almost up to the base of these leaves. This will encourage root development from the stem stock. After you have repotted the seedlings, place them within 2 in. of the fluorescent light tubes or on a sunny window sill and see if the problem is corrected.

Hardening Off

After the danger of frost has passed in your area, it's time to get your tomato seedlings ready for setting out in the garden. This is commonly called the **hardening off** stage. Hardening off tomato plants is a necessary and important step before transplanting into your garden. The seedlings have been growing in a warm environment for 6 to 8 weeks. If you transplant them directly into the garden, the comparatively hostile environment would kill the plants.

Begin hardening off your tomato plants by setting them outdoors in their pots for a few hours the first day. Place them in an area that receives only partial sun and little or no wind. Bring the plants in at night. As the days pass, increase the time you keep the plants outdoors, gradually exposing them more to wind and sun. By the end of 10 days, your tomato plants should be hardy and ready to transplant directly into the garden.

Vertical planting of tomato seedling. Remove all but two top sets of leaves then plant deeply.

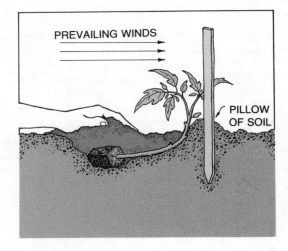

Trench planting of tomato seedling. Note the plant is buried almost to the top set of leaves.

A good alternative to daily hardening off involves the use of a coldframe. Put the seedlings directly into the coldframe after they have been indoors about 6 to 8 weeks. If the weather in your area permits, open the coldframe during the day and close it at night. During the end of the hardening-off period, leave the coldframe open day and night. The coldframe is generally easier to work with because trays of plants don't need to be moved outdoors during the day and indoors at night.

No matter which method of hardening off you use, keep a careful eye on the general condition of your seedlings. Gradually expose the delicate plants to the elements. Don't water as much as you did when the plants were indoors; this will encourage hardiness. If there is a chance of frost, bring the plants indoors or keep the coldframe closed.

Preparing a Place in the Garden

As the plants become hardy and the danger of frost lessens, it's time to think about where you're going to put the seedlings in your garden. There are several important considerations. Tomatoes grow best in well-drained soil with an abundance of organic material such as peat moss or compost. The ideal pH is 6.0 to 6.5. Work the soil with a shovel or tiller to an 8-in. depth. Work complete garden fertilizer, such as 5-10-10, into the soil before transplanting so the seedlings can get off to a good start. Select a spot in your garden where your tomato plants will get a minimum of 6 to 8 hours of direct sunlight daily—more if possible.

Once you've decided on the best location for the tomato seedlings, spend time working the soil. Water the seedlings about an hour before you plan to transplant them.

Transplanting

The best time to transplant is in the late afternoon when the soil has had a chance to warm up. A cloudy day is also good. In both cases, your intention should be to minimize the amount of direct sunlight the transplants receive the first few days in the garden. There are two basic ways of transplanting tomatoes: trench planting and vertical planting.

Trench planting involves removing all but the top two sets of leaves and burying the plant in a horizontal position up to the leaves. Don't try to bend the plant stem. Simply mound up a small pile of soil to support the plant. Trench planting encourages dramatic root development along the buried stem. The roots also develop more quickly because soil only 3 to 4 in. deep is usually much warmer than deeper soil.

Vertical transplanting is another popular method. You remove all but the two top sets of leaves and bury the plant up to this point. The main advantage of vertical planting is that the root system will be deep and closer to the moisture in the soil when the weather turns hot and dry.

CARING FOR TOMATOES

No matter which way you use to transplant, you'll also have to take steps to protect plants against insects and to provide some support.

Cutworm Protection

Install collars around each plant to prevent damage by cutworms. You can wrap the stem with a strip

To avoid damage by cutworms, install a top and bottomless can around seedling at planting time.

Staked tomato plant.

of newspaper about 1 in. below and 2 in. above the soil line to protect the plant. You can also use some container—like a paper milk carton with the top and bottom cut out—around the plant. When the tomato plants develop strong stems, these protective cutworm collars can be removed.

Supporting the Plants

At planting time you should decide if you're going to simply let your tomato plants grow on the ground or if you will support them. Determinate tomatoes—those which grow to a predetermined height, stop growing and bear fruit—generally don't need to be supported. Indeterminate tomatoes, on the other hand, will benefit from some kind of support system. You have several choices of support systems for tomatoes. The most common are staking and caging.

Staking usually means you can grow more tomato plants in a given area. The fruit will be cleaner and there will be less rot because the tomatoes are off the ground. The yield of tomatoes will generally be less than if the plants are simply allowed to ramble, but the tomatoes will be larger.

If you decide to stake your tomato plants, you should do it at planting time, before you put the seedling in the ground. Drive a 4 or 5 ft. stake about 1 ft. into the ground and about 3 to 5 in. away from where the plant will be. Put the stake on the prevailing downwind side of the plant so it will be against the stake when the wind blows it. As the plant grows, use a strip of cloth or nylon stockings to hold the stem on the stake. Tie tightly to the stake and loosely to the stem.

Caging is another popular support system. You can buy tomato cages from garden supply centers or you can make your own from concrete reinforcing wire. Cages are the simplest support system and do

have several advantages. The plants are much easier to tend. You can remove suckers, pick fruit and fertilize the plants more easily. The cage gives the plant full support because it completely surrounds it. Since tomatoes develop inside the cage, they are protected somewhat from sun scald by the foliage of the plant.

Place the cages over the seedlings at transplant time. To help your young plants get off to a good start, wrap the outside of the cage with an 8-in.-high strip of roofing paper and secure with staples. This black collar will gather heat which the new plant likes. It will also shelter the plant from drying winds. The roofing paper will have to be removed once the seedlings are established.

Protecting the Plants

Tomato plants really begin to grow when the weather warms. Until that time, however, it's important to protect the plants from a cold snap or especially cool nights. You can do this by covering each plant with some type of container in the evening. A cone of newspaper works well. Remove this covering early the next morning to prevent "cooking" the young plant. As the days get longer and warmer, you should not have to cover the plants.

As your tomato plants grow you will notice suckers developing from the main stem. Remove these by pinching them off. If you let these suckers grow, they'll develop into another big stem with its own blossoms and fruits. Pruning the suckers lets the plant devote its energy to the main stem, not new offshoots.

FEEDING TOMATOES

Your tomato plants will require water and fertilizer, and the area must be kept free of weeds.

Tomatoes grow well in cages.

Tomato sucker should be pinched off with thumb and forefinger.

Water-filled collar acts as a solar collector. It warms the soil, heats air around plant and provides humidity.

Watering

Tomatoes and most other garden vegetables require 1 in. of water in the form of rain or irrigation each week. In dry areas, they may need up to 2 in. a week during the summer growing season. Water plants thoroughly to encourage roots to seek water and nutrients deep in the soil. As a general guideline, soak the soil about 6 to 8 in. deep every four to five days for sandy soils, every seven to ten days for heavier soils like loam.

Water early in the day for best results. This will give the foliage time to dry out during the day. Wet foliage during darkness encourages some diseases in tomato plants. If you're using a drip irrigation system or a soaker hose, you can water any time. These systems deliver water directly to the soil and not on the foliage.

Fertilizing

Because tomatoes are considered "heavy feeders," they will need periodic fertilizing throughout the growing season. Use a 5-10-10 or 10-10-10 fertilizer.

Spread it around the drip line of the plant and work it into the soil about 2 in. deep. Then when it rains or you water the plants, the fertilizer becomes available to the roots. It's important to follow the label directions about application rates. Too much chemical fertilizer can burn or otherwise damage tomato plants.

Good alternatives to complete chemical fertilizers are organic fertilizers such as dried manure or bonemeal. Apply these organic materials in the same way. These fertilizers do not burn the roots or foliage of the plants.

There are also foliar fertilizers you can use, mixed with water before application. You can use these on the foliage and the fertilizer is available to the plant faster. Several types of foliar fertilizers are designed specifically for tomatoes.

Weeds are a big problem only when tomato plants are small. Remove any weeds as soon as you spot them. They will steal valuable moisture and nutrients from the soil. As the tomato plants grow, they will shade the area around the plant and kill the weeds.

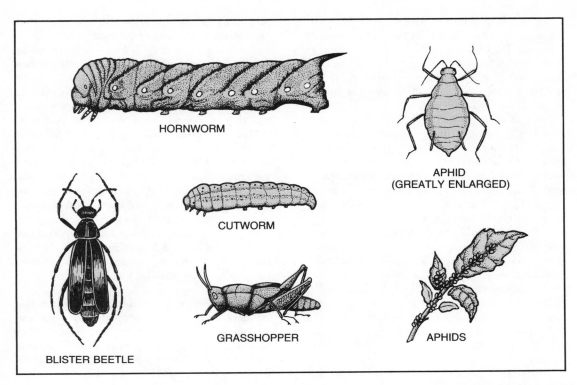

HORNWORM

APHID
(GREATLY ENLARGED)

CUTWORM

BLISTER BEETLE

GRASSHOPPER

APHIDS

Common tomato eating insects.

TOMATO PROBLEMS

There are several problems common to tomatoes. These range from a variety of diseases and insects to a general poor condition of the ripening fruit.

Diseases

Early blight is probably the most common and harmful disease of tomatoes. This is caused by a fungus that first appears as a brown spot surrounded by a yellow circle. The brown spots will appear on the lower leaves first and after these have withered and dropped, the higher leaves will show the same symptoms. Because of the heavy leaf loss, the tomato crop will usually be damaged. The most common cause of early blight is overcrowding of the plants resulting in poor air circulation. To avoid this fungus, allow sufficient space between plants—2 to 3 ft.— to encourage good ventilation. Dusting the plants with an all-purpose tomato dust is helpful. Regular use of chemical fungicide sprays such as Maneb or Zineb can also be effective. Be sure to read and follow label directions thoughtfully.

Late blight is another serious tomato plant disease. Evidence of late blight includes large brown spots on the leaves, withering and dropping of the leaves. Hard brown spots will develop on the fruit. One defense against late blight is to use a standard tomato dust such as Maneb throughout the growing season.

Leaf spot is the last common fungus disease for tomato growers. This problem will develop where warm, moist weather is prevalent—even in the cooler regions. Leaves begin to show small spots with light centers. Then they will usually turn yellow and drop off. The fungus that causes this disease lives on old tomato vines, in the soil and on perennial weeds. There are several things you can do to prevent leaf spot including rotating crops annually, spraying with a fungicide such as Zineb or Maneb, and keeping your garden free from perennial weeds.

Blossom end rot is a physiological problem in tomatoes that results in fruit with a black, watery depression on the bottom. While there are no sprays for blossom end rot, there are two good ways to keep it from happening.

The first is to make certain that the soil has an ample supply of calcium, an element found in ground limestone. The best way to determine if the amount of calcium in the soil is to test for pH. There is usually enough calcium in the soil when the pH is between 6.8 and 7.0. If the pH is above or below this level, correct as necessary.

The second way you can prevent blossom end rot is to give the plants an even supply of moisture. Weekly watering is generally not enough because much of this water will be lost to evaporation. You can help the soil hold moisture by mulching the base of the plants with hay, grass clippings or leaves. As the mulch settles and becomes thin—usually around the middle of the growing season, add more.

Sunscald is another common problem for tomatoes, particularly those grown on stakes. It's a result of tomatoes receiving too much direct, hot sunlight. Sunscald commonly starts as a yellowish patch on the tomatoes in direct sunlight. As the fruit ripens, this patch grows and will become grayish-white. One cure for this problem is not to prune too heavily. Another solution is to grow tomatoes in cages where more dense foliage will develop and prevent the problem.

Cracking of tomatoes is often preceded by a warm, rainy period. Tomatoes will develop cracks from expanding too quickly. While some varieties are resistant to cracking, the best way to prevent this problem is to provide moisture as steadily and evenly as possible.

Insects

There are several ways of protecting your tomatoes from insects. In this section you'll find explanations of the most common insects feeding on tomatoes. You will also find some suggestions for dealing with a small problem before it becomes large.

Cutworms are a common tomato problem. If you have ever seen one of these gray, brown or black worms, you know they curl up when disturbed. They live under the soil during the day, and at night these ¼- to 1-in.-long worms crawl out and chew tomato seedlings off at ground level. The best way to prevent damage by cutworms is to put some type of barrier around the young seedling plant. The two most common solutions are to wrap a strip of newspaper around the base of the seedling or to place a collar around the plant. In both cases the barrier should be at least 1 in. below and above the soil line.

Beetles, such as blister beetles, flea beetles and Colorado potato beetles, feed on tomato foliage. You can control them with rotenone, Sevin, or an all-purpose tomato dust or spray.

Aphids can be a problem throughout the season. They weaken the plant by sucking sap from all its parts. They can also spread disease indirectly as they move around on the plant. One thing you can do when you discover an aphid infestation is to use an insecticidal soap. You can also spray with malathion but that will also kill the lady bugs, a natural predator for aphids. You could try to wash off light infestations with the water pressure from a hose. A praying mantis will also rid a tomato plant of many of its aphids.

Hornworms are huge, green, caterpillar-like worms with thornlike horns on their back ends. They have a voracious appetite. Since they are a late season problem, they are usually discovered when harvesting fruit. The best thing to do when you spot one is to pick it off the plant and drop it into a can of kerosene. If you discover an infestation of hornworms, spray with organic BT or you could use Sevin, Dipel or Thuricide but these products can kill bees. Wait at least a day after spraying any chemical control before you harvest, then wash all fruit well before eating or processing.

Tomato fruitworms are season-long insects that eat tomatoes at any stage of development. You can pick the fruitworms off the plants if the infestation is not too heavy. Another plan of attack is to spray your tomatoes with an organic insecticide like BT as soon as you see these hungry worms in the garden. Sevin also works, but follow label directions carefully and don't eat fruit that has been sprayed within two days of harvest. Wash all fruit before you eat it.

HARVESTING TOMATOES

Ripe tomatoes are dramatic to look at, and when freshly picked from your garden, they taste delicious. Since tomatoes ripen from the inside out, you know you have a ripe tomato when the skin is firm and red.

In areas where daytime temperatures exceed 80°F, the red color of tomatoes will not fully develop. Instead, the tomatoes on the vine will have a yellowish-orange color. If your tomatoes are this color, it may be worthwhile to pick the fruit and place it indoors where it is usually cooler. Since picked tomatoes do not require sun to ripen fully, don't put them on a sunny window sill. The sun will burn them before they can ripen naturally from the inside out. Instead, put them out of direct sunlight, even in a dark cupboard, where the temperature is from 65°F to 70°F.

In most areas, the first frost is a light one commonly followed by two to three weeks of warm weather. When you learn that a frost is due, cover your tomato plants with newspaper tents, old bed sheets or other suitable covering. Remove the cover the next day and your plants should continue to ripen fruit. Eventually a hard killing frost will come. Before it strikes, harvest all your tomatoes so they can ripen indoors.

11

Growing Fruits

When you start thinking about growing berries, fruit trees and grapes you've reached a new plateau in gardening. These represent a certain permanence that you'll enjoy for many years.

Berry bushes and canes don't need much space to produce pounds of delicious berries all season long. Some types, such as hybrid blueberries, can even be grown in containers.

Fruit trees don't require much space. In fact, many of the dwarf varieties need only about 16 sq. ft. (a space roughly 4 ft. wide and 4 ft. long) to survive. Once planted, fruit trees need about as much care as a house plant.

Grapes have been cultivated around the world since before recorded history. Probably the most important factor for growing grapes successfully in your family garden is to choose varieties that will grow best in your climate.

BERRIES

Many gardeners avoid planting berry plants because of the erroneous feeling that the plants will take over the garden or not produce enough fruit to be worth the space and effort. This is unfortunate because there are varieties of berries that you can grow almost anywhere. New varieties produce substantial yields. You can easily control growth by careful and conscientious pruning.

For success with berries, there are several things that you have to consider:

● Plant varieties that are right for your soil and climate.

● Allow enough space for the berry patch to develop. You should have a minimum of 20 sq. ft.

● The area where you'll be growing berries should be in full sun.

You can grow most types of berries in your family garden provided, of course, you have enough space to devote to these perennial bearing fruits. Keep in mind that there is a variety of berries, and some don't require more than about 10 sq. ft. of space. A strawberry patch this size, for example, should supply a family of four with plenty of strawberries.

Blackberries

Blackberries have long been considered a pest plant in family gardens because they tend to ramble and the canes are full of thorns. While it may be true that blackberry canes do spread, they can easily be controlled by careful pruning. There are also thornless varieties available that are just as productive as the thorned varieties.

Blackberries bear fruit from about midsummer until the first frost. Since a carefully tended blackberry plant can produce a high yield of fruit, the average family garden will not need more than a few plants. Consider growing the plants on a trellis or fence.

When planting blackberry canes, place a small amount of gravel in the bottom of the hole. This will help overall drainage and increase your chances of success.

Blackberry plants have shallow roots and require ample moisture, good drainage and protection from drying winds during dormant periods. Choose a variety suitable for the general climate conditions in your area. Blackberries are ideal for locations where the climate tends to be moderate year around.

Plant blackberry plants in the spring if you live north of a line through the middle part of the United States; plant them in fall to early winter south of this line. Before planting, trim the long root stock and prune the canes to about 6 inches. Space the plants about 4 ft. apart. Put them in holes with gravel in the bottom to help drainage. Pack soil tightly around the root.

Blackberries bear fruit on canes that sprouted the previous year. After the second year, which is the only season a cane will bear fruit, the canes should be pruned and destroyed. Don't add them to your compost pile. If local ordinances permit open fires, they should be burned.

Harvest blackberries in midsummer right up to the first frost. The berries are ready to pick when they are a deep black color and come off the cane with a light touch. If you have to pull the berries off, they aren't fully ripe.

Boysenberries

Boysen, Logan, Young and Nectarberries are all similar in culture. This general class of berries is adaptable to a wide range of climates and well-suited for a family garden.

Boysenberries (and their close relatives) are cultivated in much the same way as blackberries. They are ideally suited for warmer climates and along the Pacific coast of the United States and the western coastal areas of southern Canada. Check a local nursery for the varieties suitable in your area.

Blueberry.

Blueberries

All blueberries grow well in soil that is slightly acid, pH 4.2 to 5.0. Blueberries are common in areas where there is an abundance of peat moss and the soil is slightly acid. There must also be adequate moisture and relatively cool summer weather. If you can approximate these conditions, you should have success with blueberries.

Blueberries are shallow-rooted plants that fall into one of three categories; high bush, low bush and rabbiteye. High bush blueberries reach a height of about 8 ft. and, therefore, require some type of support such as a trellis or high fence. Low bush blueberries can reach a height of 3 ft. Rabbiteye blueberries have been developed to do well in warmer climates where the other types are poor producers.

Plant blueberries when they are dormant, either in spring or fall. Work the soil carefully to a depth of about 1 ft. adding peat moss or sulfur to increase the overall soil acidity. Cut the plants back to about half their height before you plant them. Space the plants about 6 ft. apart.

You must plant at least two different varieties of blueberries for cross pollination. Since there are early, midseason and late bearing varieties, you can easily have blueberries throughout the season.

When starting blueberry plants, buy one- or two-year-old plants. After planting, pick off all blossoms for the first two years. Let the plants bear fruit for harvest on the third year. When the berries turn blue, they are in the process of producing sugar. Let them stay on the plant for about a week after they start to turn and then harvest. Protect the blueberries from bird damage by covering with netting.

Blueberry plants must be pruned during the dormant season—winter or very early spring. Remove all weak and old growth. The largest fruit will be borne on new canes.

Raspberries

Raspberries are the most delicate of the bramble berries. Because these berries bruise easily and do not transport well, they are not always available in supermarkets.

Raspberries grow best in cool climates. Generally, they do not do well where summers are hot and dry and winters are very cold.

The two basic types of raspberries are generally known as red and black. The major difference between them, aside from their color, is that red raspberries develop new canes from the root system. Black raspberries have arched canes that root at the tips, rather than from the root system itself. Red raspberries are grown most extensively in the west. Black raspberries are grown mostly in the east. While some raspberries have yellow fruit, they are the same as red raspberries.

Raspberries require plenty of moisture and well-drained soil to produce a good crop. Plant red raspberries in the early spring in cooler areas and in the fall in warmer climates. Black raspberries, because they are generally less hardy than reds, should be planted only in the spring after the weather has moderated.

Plant red raspberries 2 to 3 in. deeper than they grew in the nursery and about 3 ft. apart in rows 8 ft. apart. Plant black raspberries at the same depth as they were when you bought the plants. Never let the roots dry out between buying and planting. If your planting will be delayed for several days, dampen the roots and wrap them with an old towel or in plastic until you can put the plants in the ground.

When the shoots of black raspberries are about 3 ft. tall, prune the tips of these new canes to encourage lateral branching. These will bear fruit next year. In the early fall, fruit buds will develop. These buds will be dormant during the winter months and bear fruit the next summer. In the spring, cut back the lateral branches to five or six fruit buds.

Treat red (or yellow) raspberries differently. Let the plants grow undisturbed until the second spring after planting. When buds show green tips, remove all but three healthy canes per row to initiate lateral branches that bear fruit in midseason. Cut back everbearing raspberries to the ground in fall, rather than in spring or summer, to produce a heavy fall crop the next season.

It's important to pick raspberries almost as soon as they are ripe.

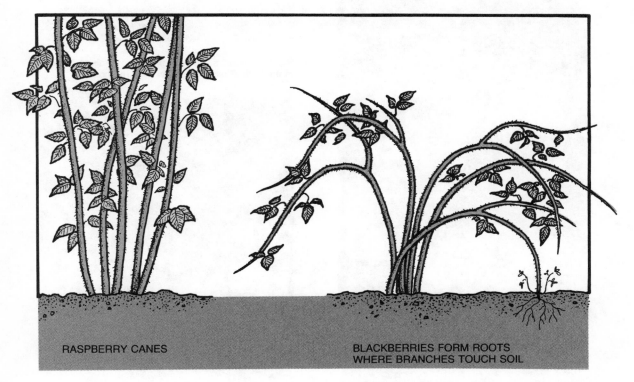

RASPBERRY CANES

BLACKBERRIES FORM ROOTS
WHERE BRANCHES TOUCH SOIL

Raspberry canes shoot up from the parent rootstock but blackberries root from the tips of growing canes.

Strawberries

Almost anyone can grow strawberries in the family garden. They are perennials and live for many years. They will bear fruit for about four years, but the first two years usually give the biggest and best yields. After this, replace the plants for best results.

Strawberry plants grow best in light-textured, well-drained soil and in a location that gets full sun. Trim the roots before planting and place them so the crown is at the soil level. Apply a 10-10-10 fertilizer about six weeks before planting.

For the greatest yields, remove most of the blossoms the first year for June-bearing strawberries. This will prevent the plants from setting fruit and will encourage it to send out runners. These will become new plants the next year. The second year you'll see a good yield from the year-old plants.

Mulch strawberry plants heavily in the fall with a 6 in. layer of hay. Because the fruit buds are dormant, you should not let them go through freeze-thaw cycles during the cold months. When the leaves lie on the ground after several frosts, cover the plants. A heavy snowfall on top of mulch will help insulate the plants.

In the early spring, a few weeks before the last frost, remove some of the mulch to see if there is any new growth. If there is, remove most of the mulch, leaving a little around the plants to discourage weeds and help the soil hold moisture. Don't fertilize or you'll encourage leaf growth before you want it.

Several types of strawberries are good for container plantings. Other types are good choices for a raised-bed strawberry patch. Check your local garden centers or nurseries for the type that grows best in your area.

Pick strawberries when they are a deep red and still firm. Use quickly or store under refrigeration no longer than a week. Strawberry jam will taste best when made with freshly-picked fruit.

Plant individual strawberry plants on a raised mound in the hole. Position roots around the mound.

Strawberries.

FRUIT TREES

Planning is the key to success for growing fruit trees. You must plant the trees according to the variety you are growing. Plant standard size fruit trees about 30 ft. apart, semidwarf trees about 15 ft. and dwarf varieties about 10 ft. apart.

You will need to plant carefully so the trees can establish a good root system. Fruit trees do best in full sun. Most soil is suitable for growing fruit trees as long as it drains well and has a pH of about 6.0. Windswept hilltops, low valleys and swampy areas are poor choices for fruit trees.

Some varieties require plantings of at least two trees for cross pollination. In most cases, one tree must be located no more than about 100 ft. from its partner.

Probably one of the greatest developments in fruit trees has been the introduction of dwarf and semi-dwarf varieties. Although dwarf trees are more expensive to buy, they take up less space and they are easier to prune, spray and harvest. Dwarf trees also bear fruit at a younger age, and the fruit is identical to that on a standard or full-sized tree.

Dwarf fruit trees are created by attaching a graft from a standard size tree onto dwarf root stock. Tree size at maturity depends on which root stock was used. A true dwarf fruit tree will reach a height of about 10 ft. when fully mature at 15 to 20 years old.

Semidwarf fruit trees are created in the same way— by grafting standard size buds onto dwarf root stock. Semidwarf trees can reach a height of about 12 to 15 ft. at maturity.

Buy your fruit trees from a reliable source. Don't buy a tree that is labeled as just "dwarf." Instead, look for the specific root stock of the tree on the label. One-year-old trees are generally preferred over trees two or three years old.

Apples

Apples are the most popular type of fruit tree grown in the home orchard. There are currently over 6000 different types. The greatest factor in choosing an apple tree is the climate of your area. Plant only trees that will endure the seasons where you live. A reputable local nursery is your best bet when buying any type of tree. Here you'll not only find apple trees suited to your area, but you will also be able to get sound advice about planting, pruning and general care of your tree.

In cooler regions, apple trees generally do better when planted in spring. In warmer climates, plant apple trees in either spring or fall. Begin planting by digging a hole larger in diameter and slightly deeper than the nursery pot or root ball. If your

Wooden branch spreader is used to force branches out at a right angle from the trunk. Check often to make certain the bark of the trunk is not being rubbed raw.

Apples are a popular fruit.

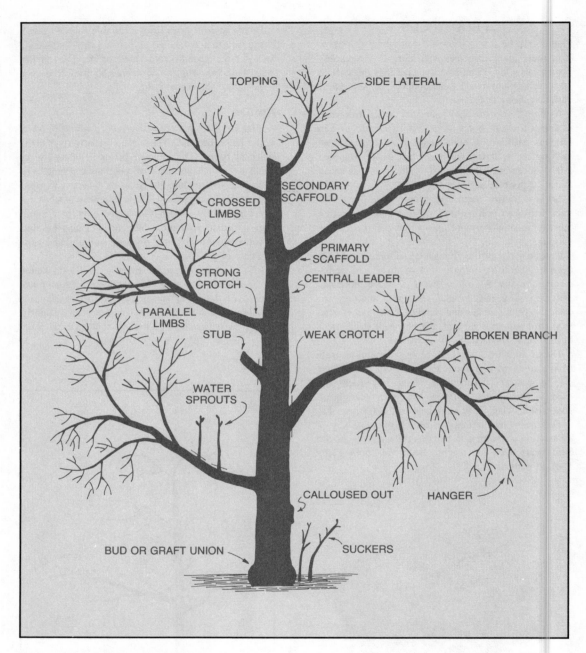

Terms used to describe types of tree branches.

soil is mostly clay, dig a much larger hole and work in plenty of organic material such as compost or peat moss. Sandy soils drain too quickly and should receive the same treatment. Work the soil so it drains well but not too quickly. You also want the soil to hold oxygen for strong root development.

Plant apple trees at about the same depth as they were growing in the nursery. Cover the roots with rich compost and topsoil. Gently pack the soil firmly in place but don't tamp it down. You may damage the root system. Water the trees well but don't apply fertilizer the first year.

Dwarf apple trees need to be staked because they have poor anchorage with their brittle roots. A heavy fruit crop may topple the tree in later years. Dwarf apple trees require support throughout their lives.

Just after planting, drive a 4-ft. long, 2×2-in. stake two feet into the ground about 6 in. from the trunk. Use a strip of cloth to tie the trunk to the stake. As the tree grows, loosen the cloth tie so it is never too tight around the trunk.

Pruning an apple tree is an art, and there are many theories about what is the proper approach. One popular way is to prune the tree during the first year or two so it will begin to develop into a proper shape. At planting time, cut the tree back to a height of 30 to 36 inches. The uppermost branch will usually develop into the central leader. During the following spring and summer check the tree at six-week intervals to make certain that one central branch continues to grow upward. Remove any narrowed angled laterals that compete with this central leader.

The first dormant pruning is important. Select three to five wide-angled lateral branches along the leader and remove all others. The lateral branches should be distributed as evenly as possible around the central leader. Think of the central leader as a wheel hub and the lateral branches as spokes. To encourage the lateral branches to grow outward at an angle of about 60° off the central leader, you can use wooden or metal spreaders. Keep these spreaders in place about two or three growing seasons. You'll also have to cut back the central leader during the first dormant pruning. Cut it back to just above the point where you want a new set of lateral branches. The last step is to cut back any strong-growing laterals so all growth is balanced. This will encourage secondary branching.

After about the third year the apple tree should start bearing fruit. When it does, cut back the central leader to a height of a short lateral branch. In succeeding years, remove upright growth during the annual dormant pruning to maintain the desired height.

When the spread of the tree is about as wide as you want, all scaffold branches are cut back to reduce a wider spread. It's important to maintain a pyramidal shape throughout the life of the tree. Prune any branches that cross or rub on other branches. Try to get good light exposure to all branches.

Apricots

Apricots can grow in most regions except in very cold or very warm areas. Apricot trees generally will not do well in areas that have winter temperatures below 30°F, but there are new varieties being developed that can withstand colder winters. Your local nursery can help you choose the best variety for your area.

Apricot trees grow best in deep, fertile, well-drained soil with a neutral pH. After the trees have been in the ground for two or three seasons, give them an application of 10-10-10 fertilizer. Also give them applications of nitrogen in spring or fall. Nitrogen deficiency causes yellow foliage with smaller and less fruit.

Apricot trees tend to produce more fruit than they should bear. You should thin the fruit during the pit-hardening stage. That's about six to eight weeks after bloom. Remove small fruit and break up clusters. The degree of thinning depends on the age of the tree, number of fruits set and the size of the fruit you want at harvest time. Fewer apricots generally mean larger fruit.

You'll have to prune apricot trees to maintain vigor and shape. Prune lightly for the first few years because heavy pruning tends to dwarf the tree. Long, slender branches require pruning or heading back to induce branching. Trees should be kept open to allow good light penetration and to form fruit-bearing branches.

Apricot fruit develops on short spurs that don't live long. Delaying pruning after bloom is often advisable. At this time you'll have a clear picture of unproductive branches. If your apricot harvest is small, prune lightly next season.

Apricots.

Cherries.

Cherries

There are two types of cherries, sweet and sour. Sweet cherries—Queen Anne and Bing are the most popular—are for eating with your fingers. Sour cherries—like Montmorency, English Morello and Early Richmode—are for preserves, jams and pies. Sour cherries are easier to grow than sweet cherries. Cherry trees generally do well in any area where apples can be grown because the climate requirements are about the same. It may take four years for a sour cherry tree to bear fruit; sweet cherries may take a year longer. Sweet cherries require cross-pollination to set fruit, so you must plant a tree of another variety nearby capable of cross fertilization.

Cherries require well-drained, slightly alkaline soil (pH 7.0 to 8.0) in full sunshine. Low lying areas, which do not drain well, are poor places to plant cherry trees. These stone fruits won't tolerate damp conditions. During the growing season, cherry trees require soak irrigation periodically. Wait for signs of moisture stress between waterings. As a rule, avoid light irrigation on a regular basis. In arid regions, regular irrigation is a must for fruit development. Cherry trees bear fruit in the third or fourth year.

Try not to prune until the tree begins to bear fruit. It's a fact that unpruned trees bear fruit a year earlier than pruned trees. Prune lightly when the tree is about 4 or 5 years old. Remove any crossing branches, dead wood and any branches (scaffolds) that prevent good sunlight penetration to the center. A popular shape with commercial cherry growers is the open-centered, vase type which lets sunlight flood the center of the tree. Thinning of the fruit is also required to increase overall fruit size and protect limbs from breaking. A cherry tree with its limbs bent to the ground may be appealing (especially at harvest time), but the fruit will be small and infested with a variety of ground-crawling insects.

You'll have to fight the birds for your cherry crop. Netting is a worthwhile investment and an effective way to protect the fruit.

Peaches

There are hundreds of different peach varieties. For success, however, you should buy peach trees from a reputable local garden center. Trees from this source will be appropriate for the climate of your area and should do well. Most peach trees pollinate themselves. To be sure you get a good crop of peaches, however, plant several trees if you have the space. Peach trees will begin to bear fruit about three or four years after planting.

Peach trees grow best in well-drained, fertile soil with a pH range of 6.0 to 8.0. Peach trees generally require winter temperatures below 40°F and summer heat for fruit development. Late spring frosts can wipe out an entire peach crop or dramatically reduce the yield. Monthly feedings of a complete garden fertilizer such as 10-10-10 will encourage strong development.

To encourage new growth, you must prune peach trees when you plant them. Cut back the central leader to a height of 2 to 3 ft. If there are scaffold branches, remove all but four which, in an ideal situation, grow out from the trunk like spokes on a wheel. Cut these back to about 4 in. long. After this initial pruning, little if any additional pruning will be necessary until the tree begins to bear fruit. Then, during the dormant period, prune to develop an open-vase shape. Pruning often results in water shoots or suckers from the base of the tree. Remove these at the soil level.

Pear.

Peaches.

Open center, vase shape pruning technique.

Central leader pruning shape.

You'll usually have to do some thinning after the fruit has begun to develop. This will result in larger fruit at harvest time. Thin peaches to about 4 to 6 in. apart.

Protect developing peaches from birds by covering with netting or tie plastic bags to limbs. When the wind blows, the bags will fill with air and scare off many of the hungry birds.

Pick peaches when they are fully ripe. Gently squeeze the fruit to find out if it is ripe. Hard fruit is not ripe, but don't let any of the fruit stay on the tree until it is overly soft. You can store peaches up to three weeks under refrigeration without any loss in quality. Longer storage usually results in internal breakdown of the flesh. Check stored fruit regularly and remove any that have begun to rot.

Pears

Pears are not self-pollinating and require a planting of at least two varieties for effective pollination. Dwarf varieties are currently available although they may cost more than standard trees. They bear fruit earlier and are generally easier to maintain. Pear trees require almost no pruning, except for shape, throughout their lives.

Popular pear varieties in warm regions include Bartlett, Spartlett, Moonglow, Seckel, Clapp's Favorite, Aurora, Gorham, Magness, Highland and

Mosc. Some hardier varieties are John, Golden Spice and Harbin Pear. Bartlett and Seckel cannot cross-pollinate each other, but other varieties can be mixed. Magness produces a poor pollen and must be planted with at least two other varieties.

As with any fruit tree, you should purchase your pear trees from a reputable local nursery. This way you can be certain that the variety you plant will be well adapted to the climate in your area.

Pear trees will do well in almost any soil as long as they have good drainage. The ideal pH range is from 6.0 to 8.0. Plant pear trees in full sunlight, not in the shade of other trees or buildings. Feeding is not generally necessary, but watch the leaves for signs of problems. Yellow-green or pale leaves usually indicate a lack of sufficient food for the tree. Apply 10-10-10 fertilizer if required.

When your pear tree begins to bear fruit, thin if the crop is too heavy. You'll get larger, better colored and higher quality fruit. Don't let pears ripen fully on the tree. Harvest Bartletts before they begin to turn yellow. Let them ripen at room temperature.

Plums

Plum trees require a winter chill to bear fruit but most will not do well in regions where the winter temperatures drop below −20°F. Some varieties however, such as Assinboine and Bounty, will withstand

Plum.

These semitropical fruits can be grown in some parts of the United States outdoors and almost anywhere in a greenhouse.

much harsher winters. As with any other type of fruit tree, purchase plum trees from a local nursery where you'll find a variety suitable for your region.

Plum varieties fall into one of two broad categories: European or Japanese. European plums generally have a wider climate tolerance than Japanese types. The most popular European varieties include Italian Prune, Stanley, Shropshire, President and French Prune. Japanese plums include Burmosa, Santa Rosa, El Dorado, Laroda, Friar and Casselman.

Most plum varieties pollinate themselves and don't require multiple plantings. Plant in the spring so the trees can establish a sound root system before fall. In warmer climates, fall planting is preferred.

European plums are best when pruned to the modified leader system. About 6 in. of vertical spacing is best for scaffold branches. Japanese plums, because they spread more, are best pruned in the open-vase or open-center shape.

Subtropical Fruits

If you live in the cooler regions of North America, the idea of picking a citrus fruit, banana, avocado or other subtropical fruit is a distant fantasy. In the southern extremes of the United States there is an area that produces many of the warm-weather fruits we enjoy from our local supermarket. In any mild-winter region from California to Florida one can easily spot citrus trees, banana trees and other fruits that are almost unreal to people from colder regions.

The information contained in this section is general and intended to serve only as an introduction to these fruit crops. You must consult other sources such as your local county extension agent for more thorough advice. If you do live in an area that can support subtropical fruit cultivation, you can find plenty of detailed local information for the asking. Good places to start are the local nurseries where you'll find not

only the right trees but also sound tactics for success. Local gardening clubs are another excellent source of information.

Many of the subtropical trees lend themselves well to container growth. For those who live in areas where killing frosts occur, a potted lemon tree inside your house is a possibility. If you have a greenhouse, and your winters aren't too severe, you may also have luck with other subtropical plants.

The subtropical citrus trees most commonly grown in containers or greenhouses include orange, lemon and lime. Grapefruit, tangelo and tangerine are outdoor trees suited only for the warm climates.

Oranges are probably the most popular citrus fruit grown in the family garden. Fruit grows on moderate size trees with a variety of ripening dates. Hamlin is the earliest, ready in November, followed by Pineapple and Navel which ripen from December to February. Valencia begins to ripen in April. In areas where 4 to 6 hours of full sun a day is available, the Tahiti orange is a good choice for the greenhouse.

Lemon trees are probably the smallest of all citrus fruit trees and are good choices for container growing. Lemons are less cold resistant than oranges. Lemon trees are commonly pruned after bearing a crop. They actively grow all year and do not have a dormant period. Some of the more popular types include Eureka, Lisbon, Villa Franca, Meyer and Ponderosa.

Lime trees are another good choice for container growing because the trees are not large. Popular varieties include Bearss, Mexican, Key, Tahiti and Persian.

Grapefruits are grown on medium to large trees that provide not only shade but also hundreds of pounds of fruit each year. Grapefruits are large and require a long ripening period on the tree. This means they must grow in a frost-free area. Popular varieties include Seedless, Duncan and Marsh.

Tangerines ripen in December and are a popular small tree. Although fairly resistant to cold, tangerines grow best in hot climates. Fancy tangerines are the common commercial type in California. Clementine is another popular type.

Tangelo is a hybrid between grapefruit and tangerine and has many of the characteristics of both parents. It is cold resistant and a vigorous grower. Popular varieties include Minneola and Orlando, which are not cross-pollinating and must be planted around other citrus trees. Also popular is the Temple Tangor which is similar to the Tangelo.

Avocados are temperamental to grow but worth the effort. Varieties from local nursery stock will be most successful. All avocados bear crops in cycles, producing a bumper crop one year and a light one the following year. Some varieties are more dependable than others. The most popular types include Anaheim, Hass, Nabel, Fuerte, Zutano, Duke and Mexicola.

Bananas grow best in full sun with lots of heat. They can be grown in a greenhouse if lots of light is available and temperatures can be kept to 60°F at night and 70°F during the day. Bananas are actually herbs that produce fleshy stalks from underground corms. Each plant grows vigorously for about eight months, bears a crop of bananas, then dies. New stalks grow from the corm to replace the stalks that have already borne fruit. Current choices include Dwarf Cavendish, Ice Cream, Valery, Grand Nain and Enano. A good greenhouse choice is the Chinese banana which grows 6 ft. tall and produces edible 5-in. bananas.

GRAPES

There are varieties of grapes that grow in even the cooler climates. Decide well in advance if you want to grow table grapes, wine grapes or a combination. Keep in mind that some varieties such as Cardinal, Flame Seedless and Perlette ripen early, while many other types such as Concord, Himrod and Suffolk Red do not ripen until midsummer or fall.

Grapes require at least five hours of sunshine a day and even more is better. In cooler areas, plant grapes along a fence or brick wall to give the plants extra radiant heat. If you're planning to have the grapes grow on a trellis, stake or pole, drive these supports into the ground before planting the vines.

A common mistake many people make is to plant grapes as fruit trees or bushes. Grape plants are vines that develop a spreading root system. When planting grape vines, bury the root and stem below the ground level, leaving only about 2 in. of stem above the soil. You'll usually have to dig a hole about 16 in. deep. Consider the entire vine a root and don't let it dry out during the first year.

The first year of growth is the only one that should grow uncontrolled. This is done so the plant can develop as many leaves as possible, enabling it to manufacture food and greatly enlarge the root system. The first winter dormant period is the beginning of your annual pruning.

The first pruning should remove all top growth except for the strongest and longest cane. If this cane is not as long as you want it to be because it hasn't reached a point where you want branching,

LEAVE ONLY TOP BUD EXPOSED

STAKE FOR TRAINING

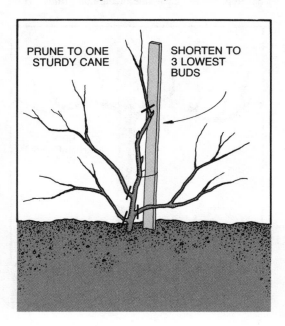

PRUNE TO ONE STURDY CANE

SHORTEN TO 3 LOWEST BUDS

Always use shears for cutting clusters of grapes off the vine—never pull them off because this can damage the vine.

Choose wine variety grapes to make your own.

cut it back to a length containing two buds. The next growing season select one vigorous shoot that is growing upright and tie it loosely with string to the support on which you're training the vine. This shoot will form the permanent trunk.

When the trunk of the vine has reached the height you want it to, cut the tip to force side branching. The next growing season, let two strong upper shoots develop, one on each side of the main trunk. Train these shoots out laterally along the trellis or other support. On the third year after planting, these side branches will send out shoots that will produce blossom clusters. These blossom clusters should be spaced about 10 in. apart. Rub off excess blossoms when they are developing to encourage plant energy to go to those that are left.

During every dormant pruning after about the third or fourth year, cut back all shoots that have borne fruit and remove all excess growth.

In cooler regions your grape vines may require winter protection from extreme cold. Do this by installing a windbreak to reduce the wind chill or by covering the vines with plastic sheeting or a straw mulch. The most important factor is choosing grape varieties that are suited for the climate in your area.

When harvesting grapes, don't remove the clusters by pulling because this will damage the vine. Use pruning tools to remove the ripe grape clusters.

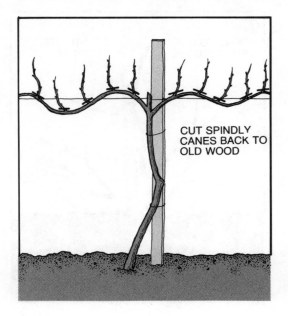

12

Flowers in the Family Garden

Flowers add color and beauty to the family garden. By picking flowers and putting them in vases around the home, you also bring this beauty indoors. Growing flowers may often be easier than growing fruits or vegetables.

The better flower gardens are well planned and cared for. Parts of your flower garden should contain a mixture of perennials, annuals and bulbs planted with an understanding of blooming times. By selecting a variety of flowering plants with a succession of bloom times, you can have flowers continuously in bloom from the first breath of spring until snow covers the garden.

Annuals are so named because they continue to flower throughout the growing season until the first killing frost. They usually don't survive the winter and must be planted new each year. Start annuals from seed or purchase them as small plants from a local nursery. The more popular types of annuals include ageratums, marigolds, petunias, poppies and zinnias.

Perennials are flowering or foliage plants whose roots live from year to year. Their tops may or may not die back in the winter. Perennials lend themselves well to sections of your garden where you want a long-lived effect, such as in a rock garden. Popular perennial types include chrysanthemum, columbine, daisies, daylilies, foxgloves, geranium, peonies and, of course, roses. Impatiens and begonias, often considered annuals, can be perennials if you let them winter indoors.

Flowering bulbs lend themselves well to permanent flower sections or borders. There are spring and summer bulbs you can plant to provide spectacular flowers from spring to fall. The most popular summer flowering bulbs include tuberous begonias, dahlias and gladiolus. The most popular types of spring flowering bulbs include narcissus, tulips, daffodils, hyacinths, iris and crocus. You can also force these bulbs to bloom indoors during the winter to add off-season color.

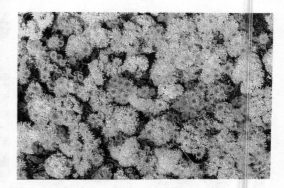

GROWING ANNUAL FLOWERS

Unless your gardening skills are high and you have a greenhouse, your best bet with annual flowers may be to purchase plants from a nursery or garden center. The time and effort required to start plants from seeds may not be worth it, especially when blooming annuals are widely available and inexpensive. If you have the tools, equipment and time, however, you can start your annual flowers from seeds in the late winter or early spring.

Preparations for Growing

Preparing the soil correctly for annuals will almost guarantee you success. If you just scratch the surface and plant, the annuals will be spindly and have a poor display of flowers. Spend some time cultivating the flower bed or border by working in organic material such as peat moss or compost and provide adequate drainage. If you do, you can reasonably expect your flower bed to flourish and produce healthy, well-developed flowers for the entire growing season.

Test your soil before planting a flower bed and adjust the pH if required. Most annuals do best in a soil with a pH range from 6.0 to 8.0. Add 10-10-10 fertilizer and work this into the soil before setting the plants. You can also get special fertilizers designed specifically for growing flowers. These are more expensive than other fertilizers but many feel the extra expense is worth the high yields of flowers.

Ageratum

Ageratum is a favorite annual flower that is ideal for edging walkways, flower beds and for container growing. Currently available are blue, purple and white varieties, all of which grow about 5 in. tall. The tiny seeds of ageratum are slow to germinate and generally must be started indoors or in a greenhouse in winter. Ageratum is available in garden centers and most people buy plants rather than start from seed.

Marigolds

Marigolds are an easy annual flower to grow in almost any family garden and are well suited for a variety of plantings. For example, walkways have greater appeal with an edging of dwarf marigolds. Marigolds have warm colors that also look good indoors and the larger varieties are good for cut flower arrange-

Petunias.

Poppies

Poppies are perennials often grown as annuals. They are self-seeding, and once established will provide flowers for many years. Popular varieties include Iceland, Oriental and California (an annual). These grow to heights of 12, 16 and 36 in. respectively. Poppies grow best in well-drained soil in full or partial sun.

Poppies.

ments. They are also useful as companion plantings in vegetable gardens because they discourage certain insects. Popular types include First Lady, Hybrid and Climax Hybrid. Marigolds flower from late spring to the first killing frost.

Petunias

Petunias are popular annual flowers. They'll bloom all season as long as you remove the spent blooms to keep seeds from forming. Petunias come in a rainbow of colors that are appropriate for bedding and container plantings as well as hanging baskets. Petunias must be started six to ten weeks before planting in the garden. As with most other annuals, petunias are widely available from your local nursery or garden center. The advantage of buying rather than starting petunias is that the flowers will be in bloom when you purchase them. You'll know exactly what colors you'll be planting.

Zinnias.

Zinnias

Zinnias are another popular annual for the family flower garden. A wide selection of zinnias is available with flowers ranging in size from 1 to 6 in. across on plants that grow from 6 to 36 in. high. You can get zinnias in almost any imaginable color except blue. The plants bloom prolifically all summer and can withstand hot, dry weather. Mildew is a common problem, especially in cool, damp climates. To eliminate or at least keep this problem in check, plant hybrids (which are more resistant to mildew), or water the plants only at ground level to keep the foliage dry.

GROWING PERENNIAL FLOWERS

Perennial flowers, once established in the family garden, will provide years of flowers for color and cutting throughout the growing season. Success with perennials requires a well-prepared seedbed, strong seed or root stock, and an uncrowded growing area. A specific area set aside for a perennial flower bed such as a rock garden is a good place for these plantings.

Preparations for Planting

Soil preparation is extremely important with perennial flowers. While annuals grow easily in almost any soil, perennials won't do well the second year if the flower bed isn't properly prepared before planting.

The flower bed for perennials must be spaded or tilled about 8 in. deep before planting. Work in or-ganic material such as compost or peat moss, and generally make the bed drain well. This will mean you will have to lighten heavy soils containing clay by adding sand as well as organic material. You could also consider raised beds or planters for your perennials.

Test your soil before planting and adjust the pH if necessary. The ideal pH range for most perennials is from 6.0 to 8.0. Add limestone to raise the pH or sulfur to lower it.

Work a complete garden fertilizer into the soil before planting. A good choice is 5-10-5 or a fertilizer designed specifically for growing flowers. Add the fertilizer on the same day you'll be planting. Add organic material to the beds each year to keep the soil in good condition.

Protection from wind that will dry or damage the flowers is also important. Winter winds can damage or kill perennials. Protect them by locating the plants carefully. They will naturally be protected simply by being on the east or south side of structures, fences or evergreen shrubbery. For other locations consider covering the flower bed with straw or other mulch after the first hard freeze. A 6-in. layer of mulch will protect the plants in subzero weather in most regions.

Summer winds can also damage perennials by drying out the foliage. You must provide adequate moisture during the growing season. Consider drip or spray irrigation if your part of the country is dry during the summer months and there is less than about 20 in. rainfall annually.

Choosing seeds or plants for your perennial flowers is simple once you decide which plants you want. Any current offering in seed catalogs is large, and new colors of established perennials seem to be introduced each year. With a wide variety of plants also sold at local nurseries, you should have little problem finding the varieties you want.

Still another way to get perennial flowers is from friends, neighbors or local gardening clubs. Some perennials such as chrysanthemum, daisy, daylily, iris and columbine, tend to take over sections of any garden. It's common practice to dig up these plantings about every five years, break up the clumps of roots and replant only about half of them. You can start your perennial flower garden from plants you get from other gardeners when they do this thinning.

With the vast selection of perennial flowers available, it would be impossible to include all choices. In this section we'll cover these popular varieties: begonia, columbine, daisy, daylily, foxglove, hollyhock, impatiens and peony.

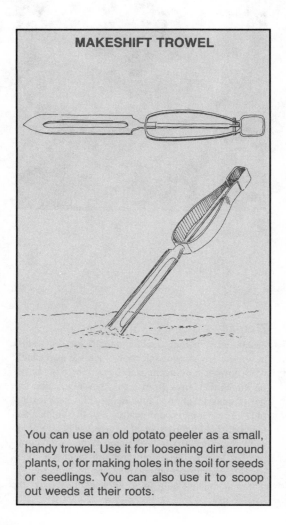

MAKESHIFT TROWEL

You can use an old potato peeler as a small, handy trowel. Use it for loosening dirt around plants, or for making holes in the soil for seeds or seedlings. You can also use it to scoop out weeds at their roots.

Begonia plants are excellent for hanging baskets.

Begonias

Begonias come in three types: tuberous, which are grown for their large, showy flowers; bedding begonias; and the rhizomes, grown for their attractive foliage. Begonias are perennials that are commonly grown as annuals. Seeds and bulbs must be started inside in winter for setting into the garden in spring. If your season is long, begonia seeds or bulbs can be planted directly in the garden when the outside temperature won't fall below 55°F. All begonias will do better in partial shade rather than full sun.

Use tuberous types for shady garden locations, hanging baskets and other containers where showy flowers will bloom until the first frost. Other types are useful for edging around flower beds and for shady areas where low-growing plants will lend a nice touch.

You can extend the time they flower by bringing the begonias indoors in the early fall when the weather begins to change. Small varieties such as Wax Wing, Strawberry and Rex make attractive house plants.

Columbine

Columbine is a popular perennial. In some areas, especially in the west, columbine grows wild in mountain ranges, deserts and coastal areas. Where permitted, you can dig up these wild plants for transplanting in your flower garden. Be sure you ask before you dig. In time, columbine can spread across the landscape like may other types of wildflower perennials.

Hybrid columbine, such as the popular Longspur Columbine, grows to a height of about 3 ft. It comes in many soft colors to add charm to outdoor plantings and to use for cut flowers. Other varieties include Alpine, Rocky Mountain and Sitka. Dwarf varieties include Alpine and Yukon Columbine.

Besides choosing varieties that do well in your climate, be sure to give your columbine well-drained, rich soil. Annual applications of compost or peat moss will almost guarantee plenty of these spurred flowers all season. Columbine will grow in full sun or partial shade.

Domestic columbine comes in many bright colors.

Wild columbine.

Daisies

Daisies are a worthwhile addition to any perennial bed. You can choose from several different varieties. The most popular daisies include Shasta, English, Gloriosa, African and Painted. While some daisies bloom only in June and July (Shasta, for example), other types will bloom all summer under the right conditions. Varieties such as the English Daisy require moist, well-drained soil and partial shade. Other daisies, such as African, Gloriosa and Painted require full sun to bloom all season.

Flower breeder Dr. Dennis Flaschenriem with Starburst Hybrid Shasta Daisy.

Daylilies

Daylilies are another favorite for the perennial flower bed. Daylilies will grow almost anywhere with full sun, but they can also tolerate partial sun. As the saying goes, "Daylilies like their heads in sunshine and their feet in shade." Hybrids are available in a range of colors including yellow, pink, rust and purple. Hybrids tend to be less invasive when compared to wild strains such as the familiar orange roadside varieties. Daylilies are a nice flower for the sunny side of a house, as a backdrop or around a tree.

Daylily.

Most daylilies grow about 3 ft. tall. New hybrids such as Triploid Daylilies have a maximum height of about 2 ft. Special soil requirements are few, as long as the area drains well. Cultivate the area well and mix in compost before setting the plants.

Older varieties of daylilies will spread over an area, choking overall growth. These older stands will benefit if you dig up all the roots, separate them and replant. A daylily bed reaches its life limit after about five years. After that there will be more foliage than flowers. Use a spading fork to break up the tangled root masses into manageable clumps about the size of a head of broccoli. Then replant them with a 2-ft. spacing. Fall is the best time for replanting daylilies. The following season you'll see more foliage growth than flowers, but in successive years you should see profuse and long lasting flowers. After another five years you'll want to break up the stand and replant the flowers.

Break up daylily root systems and replant.

Foxglove.

Hollyhocks.

Foxglove

Foxglove is actually a biennial, producing only foliage the first year. After wintering over, foxglove
will grow to about 3 to 5 ft. high. It then blooms in
June and July. The unusual flower display of foxglove
adds variety to your perennial flower garden. Color
choices include pink, rose, purple, cream, primrose
and white. Plant seeds about 2 ft. apart in a sunny
or partly sunny location. Plant seeds in the early
spring for good growth the first year.

Foxglove likes well-drained soil and a pH soil
range from 6.0 to 8.0. Because the flowering plants
(the second year) can grow to be 5 ft. tall, this flower
is best used as a background planting between shrubbery or under high branching trees.

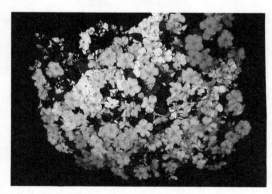

Impatiens.

Hollyhocks

Hollyhocks are about 6 ft. high. They are excellent
for planting along walls, fences and buildings. They
also make a good background planting for shorter
perennials. A wide variety of colors is available ranging from scarlet to yellow. Hollyhocks are easy to
grow in full sun, providing the soil drains well and
contains an abundance of organic material such as
compost or peat moss.

Hollyhocks require a little special care every spring
to prevent rust disease that shows up as brown spots
all over the leaves. Rust will greatly reduce the flowering potential. The best way to avoid rust is to
remove all leaves at ground level in the spring. Don't
compost these leaves but instead dispose of them
away from the garden. For added insurance, spray
the plants with agricultural sulfur, Maneb or Ferbam
every six weeks. Apply a complete garden fertilizer
in early spring and again in late summer or early
fall. Hollyhocks are self-sowing so that young plants
spring up every year. These can be dug up and re-
planted or given to gardening friends.

Impatiens

Impatiens plants are often sold as annuals, but are
perennials in frost-free areas. You can start them
from seed, use cuttings or buy already flowering
plants. Impatiens seeds are slow to germinate and
require almost greenhouse conditions for complete
success. Cuttings are a different matter. Simply snip

Peony.

off a small branch from an established impatiens and plant it in a small pot filled with a seed-starting medium. A mixture of sand, potting soil and vermiculite will be okay. In about two weeks a root system should be well established and the plant will be ready for repotting in commercial potting soil. When the plant is about 5 in. tall, pinch back the top growth to encourage branching. The plant should flower all winter indoors. In the spring, after all danger of frost has passed, move the impatiens plant into a shady location in your garden. If you follow this routine, you should be able to overwinter impatiens for many years.

Peonies

Peonies are another popular garden perennial. They are sometimes called ''Century Plants'' because once established, they bloom for a very long time. A wide variety of colors and shapes is available primarily in pink, white, bright red and combinations of these colors.

You can start peonies with root divisions you buy from seed companies, local nurseries or get from gardening friends. The root division should contain 3 to 5 ''eyes.'' When planting, these eyes must be no more than 2 in. from the surface or the plant will grow only foliage. Plant peonies in a hole about 1 ft. deep and 2 ft. across. Work in bone meal before planting. Form a hill in the center of the hole and put the root division on it. Then cover with 2 in. of soil. A full sun location is best but partial shade in the afternoon is okay.

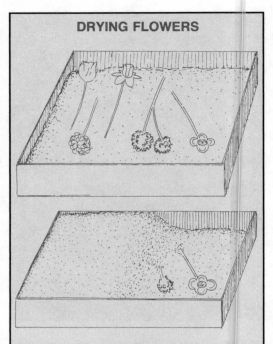

DRYING FLOWERS

In the fall, as your family gardening season is about to draw to a close, you can start a great project for your children that will preserve some of their favorite flowers from this summer's garden. Flowers like asters, chrysanthemums, marigolds and daisies are best for drying. Select some blooms from plants that have not been watered or rained on for at least two days. Choose flowers that are fresh—not too old or about to fade. Take off the leaves, being careful not to damage the flowers or stems. Get a large, flat cardboard box and cover the bottom with a ½-in. layer of cornstarch or ordinary laundry borax. Arrange the flowers so they don't touch each other and slowly sift more cornstarch or borax over them so each is covered with at least ¼-in. of the material. Keep the box in a closet for about a week and then check to see if they're completely dried. Shake the dried flowers gently to remove the cornstarch or borax. The dried flowers make attractive off-season decorations and will never need watering.

Peonies can be left indefinitely in one spot in your flower garden because they do not spread like many other perennials. If you want to expand the planting however, you must dig up the root system and carefully divide it into sections that contain eyes, then replant.

These green beans are just one of the warm-weather crops you'll find in Chapter 8.

Many garden vegetables such as tomatoes and herbs are suitable for container growing.

Growing tips for asparagus and other cool-weather crops can be found in Chapter 7.

Root crops, like these onions, are treated in Chapter 9.

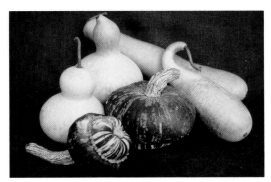

Gourds are easy to grow and make colorful decorations.

A small plot of lettuce will supply your family all season.

There are gardening tasks for all members of your family, especially for children. Give them specific jobs with almost immediate rewards and your children will learn new respect for living things and make gardening an added joy for you as well as for them.

Sweet corn is a good crop for your children to grow; the results are spectacular and the crop is tasty.

Children love to grow carrots because their efforts are rewarded a very short time after planting.

Every family garden should include flowers. In Chapter 12, you're given hints about successfully growing annual or perennial flowers and spring bulbs. There you'll also find a special emphasis on growing and caring for roses in the family garden.

Chapter 10 tells you how to grow and care for tomatoes.

The gladiolus is just one of the summer flowering bulbs.

Modern power and hand tools for the garden will make your chores easier to manage. In Chapter 3 you'll find out how to select and use these tools in your garden, and you'll be given tips on choosing the best watering device and applicator for fertilizers and pesticides.

Frames for block planted gardens are easy to build if you follow the directions in Chapter 4.

Growing this family favorite is made easy by the tips you'll find in Chapter 11.

Cucumbers provide harvests for salads all summer, and you can make pickles for the winter.

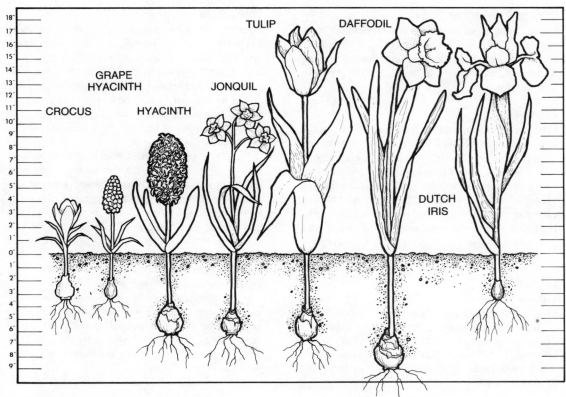

Bulb depth planting chart.

GROWING BULBS

You have a wide choice of both spring and summer flowering bulbs. Spring bulbs are generally planted the previous fall, summer bulbs as soon as the soil can be worked in the spring. Success is much easier with bulbs than with other types of flowers grown from seed or root divisions. While all bulbs like well-drained, rich loam, you can plant them almost anywhere and depend on them to bloom at least for one season.

Preparations for Planting

Container gardens in window boxes or small shallow pots are good places to plant bulbs. The advantage of having bulbs flowering in pots is that you can move the plants around to get color where none exists. Later, after the flowers have died, you can remove the plants to make room for other crops or flowers. It's important to let bulb plants grow after the flowers have died. They need the leaf growth to strengthen the bulbs for next year's growing season.

Soil conditions for bulbs present no special problems. They like a soil pH of 6.0 to 8.0. Cultivate the soil about 8 in. deep. Work in plenty of bone meal before planting. This will encourage good root growth and flower development. Planting depth of all bulbs is important. It is generally accepted that the proper planting depth is three times the height of the bulb being planted.

Naturalizing bulbs is the term used to describe a bulb garden or individual plantings of bulbs left to grow unattended. In fact, this is probably the most effective approach. One important need must be met for overall and extended growth: After flowering, the foliage of many bulbs such as crocus, daffodil and grape hyacinth must be allowed to die back naturally so the energy can be sent to the bulb for good growth the following season. You can hide the dying foliage with strategically placed annuals, removing the foliage only after it is dry and brown.

Spring Flowering Bulbs

Spring flowering bulbs include crocus, daffodil, hyacinth, iris, narcissus and tulip. These should be planted in the fall for flowers the following spring. A dormant period where the bulbs are cold is necessary for growth.

Crocuses

Crocuses are commonly the first flowers of spring. They can often be seen pushing up green foliage through the snow. The bright flowers of purple, yellow, white and striped combinations are clear indicators that soon you will be working in the garden again. A planting of crocus bulbs in the fall will give you years of early bloomers with little work. Each year will see new additions to the crocus area and in time you may want to dig them up and replant them.

Daffodils

Daffodils trumpet the arrival of spring by sending up flowers shaped like brass horns. Daffodils are great in seemingly unplanned plantings, especially on the edges of woodlands and fields. The current offering of daffodils includes yellow, white, green and combinations. Daffodils lend themselves well to naturalizing.

Hyacinths

Hyacinths are a less common spring flowering bulb, but a popular one, nevertheless, with blooms during late April and early May. Hyacinths can rightly be considered "towers of flowers." Each stem, in classic varieties, is studded with star-shaped flowers. Popular colors include red, white, pink, purple and yellow. **Grape hyacinths**, as their name suggests, are short cone-like bunches of flowers colored and shaped like purple grapes.

Hyacinths can also be forced to bloom indoors almost any time during the cold months. Not only are the flowers beautifully long-lasting, but they also fill the room with a pleasant fragrance. They do, however, require a cooling off period before you can achieve much success. The bulbs must be kept at a temperature of about 40°F for about 14 weeks. You can put them in a cold storage room or even the crisper bin in your refrigerator to make the bulbs think winter has come and gone.

After winterizing the bulbs, simply place them in a growing container and fill with gravel, rocks or soil. The root systems will develop with little care other than light waterings. After the leaves are about 1 or 2 in. long, place the pot in a sunny location until the flowers bloom.

Daffodils are a good choice for naturalizing.

Grape hyacinths.

Forced bulbs brighten indoor settings during cold winter months.

Cut off iris leaves before first killing frost.

Iris

Iris is another popular springtime flower that lets you know warmer days are coming. Iris grows from rhizomes which are large, shrimp-like roots. About five years after the initial planting, you'll have to dig up the iris area and replant. Each rhizome will have grown into a crowded and packed clump that has to be divided. You'll probably have many more "Y" shaped roots than you need so consider giving some to a friend. Check the growth for damage by the iris borer.

Before replanting the iris rhizomes, work organic material and bone meal into the bed. It's important that the area drain well and have a pH range from 5.0 to 6.0, slightly acid.

The established bed requires some periodic attention. After the flowers have died, remove the stems. Let the foliage grow until fall, then cut the leaves about 4 in. above the ground. The following spring, cover any sections of the rhizomes that may have popped through the surface.

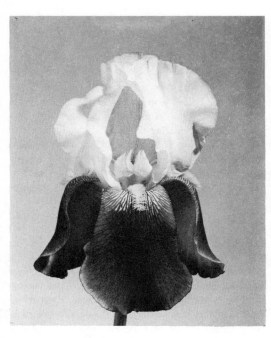

Iris.

Iris rhizome resembles an insect.

Tulips

Tulips are a favorite of gardeners in cooler regions around the world. There is a rainbow of colors available. Tulip bulbs must go through a dormant period where temperatures are below 40°F for at least 14 weeks before they will bloom. This is why tulip bulbs are planted in the early fall and allowed to overwinter in the ground.

Careful planning as well as careful planting are the keys to success with tulips. Choose colors that contrast with surrounding foliage and shrubbery. Most people prefer to have groupings of the same color rather than dots of mixed colors. Prepare the tulip bed by first cultivating it about 8 in. deep. Work in compost or peat moss and bone meal before placing the bulbs. Test and adjust the pH of the soil. The ideal pH range for tulips is from 6.0 to 7.0, neutral. Then, use a bulb planter to dig individual holes. Plant at a depth of about three times the width of the bulb. Cover with soil and water. This will enable the bulbs to establish root systems for the following spring.

The leaves help gather energy for next season, so it's important not to disturb the plants until they

Plant spring flowering bulbs in the late fall. Lay out bulbs in rows then use bulb planting tool to plant them. Sprinkle about one tablespoon of bonemeal in the bottom of each hole, add about an inch of soil, then the bulb.

Tulip.

turn brown and die back. After the leaves die, you can dig the bulbs, trim off the leaves and store for planting in the fall. Store bulbs in paper bags in a cool area until planting time.

Tulips can also be forced indoors during the cold months. Some varieties are better suited for forcing than others. If in doubt, look for tulips marked "for forcing" and buy the largest, healthiest looking bulbs you can find. When placing the bulbs in a pot for forcing, remember to keep the pointed tip up and at the soil line. Tulip bulbs also have a flat and rounded side. A large leaf always grows from the flat side so place the bulbs in the pot so that all flat sides face out. When the bulbs grow, the foliage will surround the edge of the pot and the flowers will be in the center. Use sand, soil or gravel to hold the bulbs in position. The plant gets its nourishment from the bulb, not the soil, so this material is only for support.

Narcissus

Narcissus is another popular spring flowering bulb. Oddly enough, more paper white narcissus are forced to bloom indoors than in the garden. This is easy because all the energy necessary for flowering is contained in the bulb, and all you have to do is to pot the bulb, water it and put in on a sunny window sill. It usually takes about 6 to 8 weeks for the flower to bloom. You can plant several narcissus bulbs in a single pot for an attractive and fragrant display. If you plant pots of narcissus in November, you'll have fresh flowers for the winter holidays—a great gift idea.

Summer Flowering Bulbs

Summer flowering bulbs produce flowers throughout the warm months right up until the first frost. The three most popular and easy to grow are tuberous rooted begonias, dahlias and gladiolus.

Begonias

Tuberous rooted begonias are almost without equal in shady sections of the garden. Color choices include red, yellow, salmon, orange, pink and white. Flowers can be single, double, frilled or picoteed (flowers of one color with edges of another color). These begonias grow either on 16-in.-high stems or on trailing arms which are ideal for hanging baskets or other planting containers.

Dahlia.

Tuberous begonia.

Tuberous rooted begonias are grown from rough-textured brown bulbs about the size of plums. The concave side of the tuber is the top, the rounded side the bottom. Plant tubers about 8 to 10 weeks before the last expected frost date. Begin by filling a pot almost to the top with soil that will drain well. Put the tubers in the pot and just cover with potting soil. Soak with water and let it drain. Don't water again until the surface is dry. Keep the growing plants in a warm location and in filtered sunlight. Set plants outdoors after all danger of frost has passed.

In warm regions, tuberous rooted begonias can be planted directly outdoors in a partially sunny area. Keep the soil moist but not soggy. Feed the plants with a slow-release complete fertilizer.

After the first killing frost of fall, dig up the tubers and let them air dry for a few days. Then cut back the foliage and store the bulbs until planting time again the following season. When properly cared for, the tubers will live and produce beautiful flowers for many years.

Dahlias

Dahlias like a sunny, warm location. In fact, they are the national flower of Mexico. A variety of petal formation in every color except blue is available. Dahlias make excellent flowers for the garden as well as for cutting.

Dahlia bulbs are planted directly in the garden about a week after all danger of frost has passed. Cultivate the soil about 8 in. deep, working in organic material and a complete time-release fertilizer. Plant the tubers about 4 in. deep and 2 to 3 ft. apart, depending on the expected size of the mature plant. The growing plants love full sun and hot weather. Dahlias will also grow in containers.

In the warmer regions, where there is no danger of the tubers freezing, dahlias can be left in the garden all winter. In cool areas, however, you must dig them up and store them for the winter. After frosts have killed the foliage, cut off at the soil line and carefully dig up the tubers. They will be in clumps. Let them dry for a few days, then place them in storage. The best way to store dahlia tubers is in moist peat moss, sawdust or perlite. Use a pail or other suitable container and put them in an area that stays reasonably cool and moist throughout the storage period. The following spring, take the tubers out of storage and replant.

Gladiolus

Gladiolus are tall, spike-like flowers that are grown from corms. Each spike will contain from 8 to 26 florets. A dazzling color choice is available from seed suppliers as well as from local nurseries and garden centers.

Gladiolus.

The concave side of the gladiolus corm, which is sometimes erroneously called a bulb, is the bottom but the plant will grow even if you put it in upside down! Gladiolus can reach a height of about 5 ft. and will put out a show of florets for about 10 days.

Plant gladiolus corms at a depth of about three times their width in cultivated garden soil. Work bone meal into the soil before planting and space the corms about 4 in. apart. To have a good display of gladiolus all summer, begin planting corms after all danger of frost has passed, and make successive plantings about once a week until mid summer.

After the first killing frost, gladiolus corms must be dug up and stored at 40°F to 50°F. If the corms freeze, they will die. Carefully dig the corms and cut the foliage back to about ½ inch. Let them dry in a warm, well-ventilated place for a few days. Gladiolus corms will often generate new cormels (small pea shaped corms) and some corms larger than the original. These should be separated from the parent before storing. Discard any corms that are obviously dried and dead. Store the healthy corms in an area that has a constant temperature (40°F to 50°F is an ideal range) until spring planting time.

ROSES

Roses have been a popular garden plant for centuries. They grow wild almost anywhere. Most commercial roses have a bit of Southern China in their ancestry. For this reason they must be protected during the very cold months.

Roses are a popular garden flower.

Types of Roses

Roses can be classified as bush, climbing or hedge types.

Bush roses are grouped into types according to their flowering habit, winter hardiness and other characteristics. The types of rose bushes are floribunda, grandiflora, polyantha, hybrid perpetual, shrub, old-fashioned and tree (standard or miniature).

Climbing roses include all varieties that produce long canes and require some sort of support to hold the plants off the ground. Climbing roses are hardy and are becoming more popular for landscaping as new varieties become available. Climbing roses, like bush roses, fall into several types, and there is much overlapping so one variety can actually be included in one or more listing. These types are generally available: rambler, large-flowered climbers, ever-blooming climbers, climbing hybrid teas, climbing polyanthas, climbing floribundas and trailing roses.

Rose hedges make an attractive natural fencing material or screen for your garden. When you use roses, however, they take up more space than the plants usually used for hedges and they do lose their leaves in winter where other hedge plants may not. Plant the roses closer together than you would in the garden. Regular pruning is necessary to keep the hedges under control. Rose varieties that generally make good hedges include the rugosas, gallica roses (for a lower, more colorful hedge), and some of the floribundas.

Buying Roses

Buy roses from a reputable source such as a local nursery or garden center to ensure you'll get high quality plants. There are also dependable mail-order sources that will guarantee plants, besides showing the blooming flowers in a catalog so you'll know what to expect. Local gardening clubs are another good source of not only plants but also information about the varieties that will do well in your area.

Growing Conditions

Roses grow best in full sun, but you can also plant them where they'll receive at least six hours of sun daily. If you're considering a partial sun location, remember that morning sun is better than afternoon sun. Morning sun will help dry dew off the foliage and reduce the chances of leaf diseases. Roses do best when planted by themselves away from other types of flowers.

The ideal planting time for roses is determined by the part of the country you live in and the severity of the winter. Here are some general guidelines:

● If winter temperatures do not go below 10°F, plant roses at any time the plants are fully dormant.

● If winter temperatures commonly fall below 10°F, plant roses only in the spring.

● If you are planting roses purchased in containers, you may plant them any time from spring to fall.

When planting rose bushes singularly or in groupings, cultivate the soil about a foot deep. Work in plenty of organic matter. Test the soil and adjust the pH, if necessary, to the ideal range of 5.5 to 6.5. If you're planting a single rose bush, dig a hole at least 1 ft. deep and 18 in. wide. Work a shovelful of well-rotted manure into the bottom of the hole and cover it with soil so the growing roots won't come in direct contact with the manure.

Planting Roses

Just before planting, unwrap the root system and prune off any dead or injured roots. Remove any dead or broken canes, and cut the canes back. Depending on the rose bush and the region you live in, the recommended length of the stems you cut back can be anywhere from 4 in. to about 12 in. long. Make your cut no more than ¼ in. above an eye or growth bud.

As you inspect the bush before planting, note the location of the bud union. The bud union is the weakest part of the plant, and it shows where the flowering stock has been joined to a vigorous root stock. The future success of the rose depends on the union being planted at the proper depth.

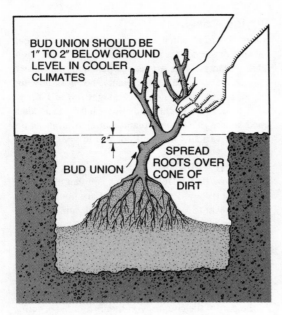

BUD UNION SHOULD BE 1" TO 2" BELOW GROUND LEVEL IN COOLER CLIMATES

2"

BUD UNION

SPREAD ROOTS OVER CONE OF DIRT

Plant rose bush on mound in bottom of hole.

If winter temperatures in your area fall below 20°F, plant the bush so the bud union is 1 to 2 in. below the soil surface. If winters are mild, plant with the bud union about 1 in. above the soil line. When the bud union is above the soil level, new canes grow more freely. Many gardeners in colder climates compromise better new growth with winter protection by covering the bud union with soil or thick mulch in the fall to protect against damage over the winter.

In the bottom of the planting hole, make a cone-shaped pile of soil. Set the rose bush on top of this and spread the roots down the slope.

Carefully work soil around the roots so that they are in contact with the soil. After you have covered the roots, pour about a gallon of water into the hole to help settle the soil. After the water drains, fill the hole with more soil.

As the bushes grow, remove weeds regularly, being careful not to damage any roots that may have worked toward the surface. Apply mulch to keep the soil damp around the plants.

Roses need fertilizer after the new spring growth is well established and all danger of frost has passed. You can make a second application of rose food fertilizer later if the plants show evidence of mineral deficiencies. Yellow leaves indicate a lack of nitrogen; grayish-green leaves indicate a lack of phosphorus; and browning leaf margins indicate a lack of potassium or possibly a lack of water. Use only fertilizers that are designed and labeled for roses. Don't apply fertilizer after July 15 in cold climates or after August 15 in mild climates.

Cutting and Pruning Roses

There is nothing quite like a vase of fresh cut roses for beauty and fragrance in the home. Cut roses should last for almost a week, but sometimes they will wither within a day or two after cutting. Often you can revive cut roses by making a slanted cut an inch up from the bottom of the stem. Plunge the end of the stem in almost-boiling water for a few minutes, then dip the ends quickly into cold water. The hot water drives off any air bubbles in the stem so that cool water can rise up and revive the flower.

There are several things to keep in mind when you cut your roses. Use only sharp cutting shears; never rip off the flowers. Make a clean cut about ¼ in. above the top group of five leaves on the stem. Roses cut just before the petals begin to unfold will live longer as cut flowers than roses that have fully opened. Some people suggest that roses should not be cut in the first year of growth. Others claim that cutting roses when the blossoms begin to fade prevents the bush from setting seeds, increasing the overall output of flowers.

Rose bushes require annual pruning to improve appearance, remove dead wood and generally improve the quality and quantity of the flowers. If you don't prune them, you'll have a bramble patch over time with small, rather poor flowers.

Use sharp tools for pruning. You'll need pruning shears and possibly loppers for thick cane stock. You'll want to cover the freshly cut areas with some sort of a sealer to protect against the cane borer. While there are commercial products available for this, white carpenters glue works just as well—and is cheaper. Don't use sprayers in aerosol cans because you don't want to cover any of the buds.

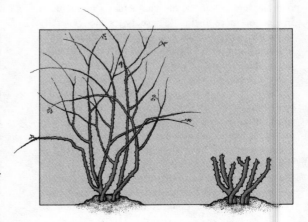

Prune rose bushes to encourage new growth.

Bush roses are pruned in the early spring before new growth begins. Start by removing all dead wood, making your pruning cut about an inch below dark colored areas. If there are no buds, remove the entire cane. If two branches cross, remove the weaker one. Cut out all weak growth and any canes that grow toward the center.

Climbing roses should be pruned just after they have flowered. This will stimulate new cane growth which will produce next year's flowers. Shorten the strong, vigorous canes to stimulate laterals to develop. In the spring, prune climbing roses only to remove dead or damaged canes. Heavy pruning then will reduce the overall production of flowers.

Remove suckers on any roses as soon as you see them. Suckers are stems that grow from the roots below the union. You're better off pulling these off the roots because cutting could just encourage further growth—as if they were pruned.

Don't compost any of the rose canes you prune off. Dispose of them in other ways.

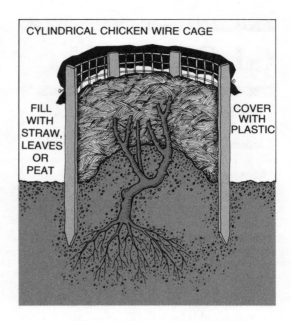

In cold areas, cover rose bush with wire cage filled with straw. Cover top of container with black plastic.

Winter Protection

Roses require winter protection not only from low temperatures but also from fluctuating temperatures which do even more damage to the bushes. Healthy plants stand a better chance of surviving cold than bushes that are in poor condition at the onset of cold weather.

In the colder regions, don't feed (fertilize) roses later than mid July. Don't prune them in the fall; this would encourage new growth that would only be killed by the cold. Let flowers mature into seed pods (rose hips). This seems to help the bush go into a dormant period. Cover the bases of rose bushes with about 12 in. of mulch to protect them from the cold. In very cold regions, you may need to cover the entire bush with mulch. Local gardening clubs are a good source of more specific information to help guarantee you success with roses in your area.

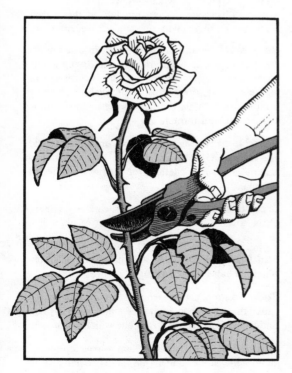

Always use pruning shears for cutting roses. Never rip flower off the vine.

PROTECT PLANTS FROM HOSE DAMAGE

To keep a hose from breaking plants when you water the garden, place a piece of 1×2 lumber or a large stick in the ground at the corner of the garden. This will hold the hose away from the plants when you pull it to do your watering.

GLOSSARY

Absorption Assimilation of molecules or other substances into the physical structure of a solid or liquid without any chemical reaction.

Acid Soil Soil with a pH below 7.0. Some garden plants such as carrots, lima beans and peppers, grow well in soil that is slightly acid. These examples grow best in soil with a pH of 6.0 to 6.5. Acid soils occur naturally in the East, largely from the decaying of leaves. Acid soils may be neutralized by adding ground limestone.

Aeration Process of loosening soil to increase air circulation within the soil.

Air Layering Technique of propagating plants by inducing root formation at a point along the stem. The most common method used for this is to partially sever the stem, keep the cut open with sphagnum or peat moss and cover it with a plastic bag until roots form. When roots develop, the stem is cut through and the new plant is removed and planted.

Alkaline Soil Soils with a pH reading above 7.0; it's the opposite of **acid** soils. Alkaline soils are most common in the West, but can be caused by overliming acid-type soils. To neutralize alkaline soils, agricultural sulfur is applied. Some plants grow well in soils that are slightly alkaline. These include asparagus, lettuce, turnips and peas.

Alum Common name for aluminum sulfate, used to acidify neutral or alkaline soils.

Annuals Plants which grow from seed, flower and produce seed in one year and then die.

Aphids One of the most common garden (and houseplant) insects. These sucking insects are usually found on the undersides of leaves and on plant stems.

Asexual Reproduction Propagation of plants through grafting, cutting, budding, air layering, etc., where growing tissue rather than a seed is depended upon to produce a plant.

Assimilation Ability of a plant to take nutrients and transform them into plant tissue.

Available Plant Foods Nutrients that can be used by growing plants.

Backfill Returning soil to a planting hole after the root system of a plant has been positioned in the hole.

Bare Root Plants Deciduous trees and shrubs with all soil removed from the root system and sold during the later winter and early spring. These plants are in the dormant stage and root systems must be protected from sunlight, wind and damage. Bare root plants should be put in the soil as soon as possible after purchase.

Bedding Plants Annual plants that are sold in bulk for planting in flower beds and borders.

Biennial Plant that completes its life cycle in two years. Seeds are planted in spring, plants grow for one season, go dormant, and the following spring and summer they bloom, set seeds and die.

Blanching Process of depriving a plant of light to produce a pale, tender plant. This is commonly done with cauliflower, celery, endive and other plants.

Bloom Stalk Stem that bears a plant's flower or group of flowers.

Bolt Vegetables and annual flowers which have prematurely flowered before full development. This is a common problem when hot weather arrives too early or plants are set out too late in the season. Bolting is a problem with spinach, lettuce and celery.

Bone Meal Organic fertilizer, high in calcium and phosphorus, made from grinding and drying animal bones. Bone meal is a good soil additive when planting bulbs; it dissolves slowly to prevent burning the plant tissue. It safely encourages maturity, blooming and aids in seed formulation.

Broad Leaf Having broad leaves instead of needle-like leaves. A broad-leaf weed is any weed which is not a grass. A dandelion, for example, is a broad-leaf plant.

Broadcast To scatter material, such as seed or fertilizer, over a broad area rather than to place it in rows.

Bud Undeveloped shoot, stem or branch of a plant which includes flowers or tightly curled leaves.

Budding Propagation technique where a single bud rather than a branch is grafted onto another plant. Budding also refers to a flower bud which has opened.

Bud Union That part of a plant where top growth joins with stock under the soil, roughly 1 to 3 in. above the rootstock. It is the large mass from which stems grow.

Bulb In common usage, any plant that grows from an onion-like globe. Examples include onion, tulip and amaryllis.

Burning Usually a result of improper or overapplication of commercial fertilizer causing reverse flow of sap from the plant.

Calcium Major plant food which aids in the formation of plant cells. Calcium is generally applied to soil as calcium carbonate (limestone) or as a component of a complete fertilizer.

Caliche Commonly found as a deposit (calcium carbonate or lime) below the soil line in the Southwestern United States.

Cambium Layer of living tissue in plants just below the bark. Its growth results in the increase in thickness of stems and roots. It is, for example, the only living tissue in the trunk of a tree.

Carbon Important element in the structure of all plants, equaling about one-half of the plants' dry weight. It is obtained primarily from atmospheric carbon dioxide.

Chlorophyll Green pigment in plants.

Chlorosis Condition when plant foliage turns pale or yellow. It is caused by a lack of iron, nitrogen, sulfur or magnesium in soil.

Clay Soil composed of tiny mineral particles that are densely packed. Clay soil does not drain well, feels greasy when wet, and becomes brick-like when dry. Greater amounts of lime or sulfur are required to bring about a pH change in clay soils. Clay soils are commonly referred to as **heavy soils**.

Coldframe Low structure with glass or clear plastic top used to protect plants outdoors from cold temperatures.

Cole Crops That family of vegetables which grows well in cooler temperatures including members of the cabbage family: broccoli, Brussels sprouts, cabbage, kohlrabi and cauliflower.

Companion Crops Crops which have a different harvest date but are grown in the same section of a garden. Early ripening crops are harvested leaving room for later ripening crops, making optimum use of garden space. Companion planting also refers to the practice of placing one plant near another for certain beneficial effects. For example, onions planted near roses will help deter infestations of some insects.

Compacted Soil Soil that has been naturally or mechanically pressed down to form a tight mass. Compacted soil must be cultivated to introduce air and water before planting.

Complete Fertilizer Plant food that contains the three major elements of plant growth—nitrogen, phosphorus and potassium.

Composite Family Large family of plants that includes all flowers known as daisies. Other examples include dahlias, marigolds and zinnias.

Compost Mixture of soils and organic waste materials—leaves, plants, kitchen scraps, manure—which are allowed to decompose. The result is a rich and safe soil amendment for use in a garden. The material must be kept moist and turned periodically to encourage thorough decomposition.

Conifer Evergreen family of plants including pine, fir, cypress and juniper. While some members such as larch are not green year round, they all produce seeds in a conelike structure.

Crop Rotation Practice of alternating crops in a garden to avoid the plant's taking the same food elements out of the soil year after year.

Corm Bulb-like underground stem from which grow leaves, roots and flowers. Gladiolus, crocus and bananas are three plants that grow from corms. A corm differs from a bulb in that food is stored in the solid center, whereas a bulb's food is contained on outer scales.

Cover Crop Often referred to as "green manure." Cover crops are planted in early spring or fall. They help to return valuable organic material and nitrogen to the soil. Common cover crops are clover, cow peas and vetch.

Cross Pollination Transfer of pollen between similar plants for the purpose of fertilization. Apple trees, for example, require cross pollination to bear fruit. Cross pollination is done by wind, birds, insects and people.

Crown That portion of a plant at the junction of the root and stem or at the root and trunk.

Cultivate Working soil with garden tools to remove weeds and generally break up the surface to introduce oxygen and help the soil drain well.

Cuttings Parts of a stem or root which are encouraged to form new roots and new plants by placing in a suitable rooting medium.

Damping Off Plant disease caused by fungi in soil. It makes seedlings wither and die after they emerge.

Deciduous Any plant that sheds all of its leaves once a year, most commonly in the fall.

Decomposition Decay, usually of strawy manure, compost or some similar substance.

Deficiencies Partial or total lack of necessary plant foods in soil or plant tissue.

Depletion Removal of necessary plant foods from the soil by the leaching action of rain water and by normal plant growth. Valuable plant foods must be replaced by adding compost or complete fertilizers before introducing new plantings.

Dieback Death of a plant stem which started at the leaf edges. There are many causes.

Division Method of plant propagation by separating an established planting. Examples include daylilies, iris, tulip bulbs and strawberry runners.

Dormancy Period during which a plant makes no active growth. Most plants are dormant during the winter season.

Drainage Term used to describe a soil condition in which water is allowed to run off or deeper into the soil and not collect to drown the plant roots.

Drip Irrigation System of providing low water presure moisture to growing plants at the root zone over a long period.

Drip Line Imaginary circle around a plant directly under its outermost branches where rain water would drip from the leaves.

Dwarf Any plant that grows smaller than its usual size, but which is nevertheless vigorous—not stunted.

Earthing-up Mounding of soil around the base of growing plants, often called **hilling up**.

Erosion Wearing away of top soil by wind, water or wave action.

Evergreen Any plant that never loses all of its leaves at one time. An evergreen plant *does* lose its leaves annually—but never all at one time.

Eye Underdeveloped bud on a tuber that will sprout after planting.

Fertilize To apply nutrients to the soil or plants. To fertilize a flower is to apply pollen (the male element) to a flower's pistil (the female element) to set seeds.

Flat Shallow plastic or wooden container used for starting seeds or growing seedlings.

Forcing Growing plants to maturity at a time that is not the normal season.

Friable Soil Soil that is light, rich and easily worked with garden tools. Soil that crumbles easily.

Frond Leaves of ferns and the leaves of palms.

Fungicide Product used to prevent or retard the growth of fungus.

Germination Sprouting of a seed after planting or soaking in water.

Grafting Process whereby a portion of a plant (scion) is made to unite with and grow on another plant (stock). The scion remains true to its characteristics as does the stock, combining the characteristics of both parent plants.

Gypsum Calcium sulfate, a fertilizer source of calcium and sulfur.

Harden Off Adapting plants which have been grown under controlled indoor conditions before setting them out in the garden. This is done by gradually exposing the plants to the elements.

Hardy Term used to describe a plant's resistance to, or tolerance of frost or freezing temperatures. For example, a plant may be described as ''hardy to −20°F'' which means it can withstand winter temperatures to this limit.

Heaving Lifting of plants caused by action of the soil during freezing and thawing cycles. Sandy soils do not heave much but clay soils can heave dramatically.

Heeling In Storing of plants in trenches or low lying structures, covered with soil or compost, until conditions permit proper planting.

Herb Generally any plant that is grown for its flavor, fragrance or medicinal properties.

Herbaceous Any nonwoody plant that dies to the ground after the growing season and that sends up new shoots the following season. It can be an annual, perennial or bulb.

Herbicide Any chemical that is used to destroy undesirable plants or vegetation.

Hilling Up Mounding soil around the base of growing plants.

Humus Well decomposed vegetable and animal material (manure) which contains a large amount of plant nutrients and moisture.

Hybrid Plant that results from crossing two plants which have different characteristics.

Hydrated Lime Used to reduce soil acidity. It is also known as **slaked lime**. It is a product of quicklime which has been treated with steam or water.

Hydroponics Growing of plants in liquid solutions of nutrients rather than soil.

Inorganic Nonliving matter such as rocks, clay or sand. Also used to describe chemical fertilizers, pesticides and similar products.

Insecticide Product used to eliminate or control insects.

Insoluble Term used to describe materials that do not dissolve in water.

Irrigation To apply water to soil when rainfall is insufficient to sustain plant growth.

Lateral Buds Growth buds on the sides of plant stems.

Leaching Removal of valuable chemical elements in the soil when water passes through the soil.

Leaf Burn Damage to plant leaves by sunlight or chemicals.

Lime Chemical compound containing calcium that is commonly used as a soil pH adjustment to raise the overall pH level. **Limestone** is calcium carbonate, **quicklime** is calcium oxide and **slaked** or **hydrated lime** is calcium hydroxide.

Loam Class or texture of soil which contains small amounts of sand, clay and silt. Loam soils generally contain large amounts of organic material.

Magnesium Important plant food that encourages the assimilation of phosphorus by the plants.

Marl Soil deposit containing calcium carbonate used for liming acid soils.

Mulch Natural or artificial material placed around growing plants to help retain moisture and to control extremes in temperature. Examples include straw, sawdust, leaves, paper and plastic.

Nematode Microscopic, transparent worm which decomposes organic matter. Nematodes in certain conditions are harmful, others are beneficial.

Neutral Soil Soil with a pH of 7.0. Neutral soil tends to become acid with moisture, alkaline with dryness.

Nitrate Chemical salt of nitrogen which is readily available to plants.

Nitrogen One of the three major elements necessary for plant growth.

Organic Matter Generally refers to any material that is derived from plants and animals.

Organic Fertilizer Any product derived from vegetable or animal sources.

Peat or Peat Moss Partially decomposed mosses that are highly water retentive and slightly acid.

Perennial Any nonwoody plant that lives for more than two years. Usually growth above soil line dies back during cold weather.

Pesticide Any chemical used for the control or elimination of garden pests. Pests can be insects, unwanted plants, plant diseases or vertebrates (like animals, birds or fish).

pH Degree of acidity or alkalinity of soil.

Phosphorus One of the key elements needed for plant growth, essential for the production of fruits and seeds. Also promotes good root development and strong plant cells.

Photosynthesis Process by which green leaves manufacture needed materials from carbon dioxide in the air, water and nutrients in the soil.

Pinching Simple pruning technique used to force side growth of a plant. Pinching tomato suckers with thumb and forefinger is commonly done to encourage growth of the main branch.

Plastic Mulch Sheet plastic, commonly black, laid on the soil surface to discourage weed growth, retain moisture and to warm the soil.

Pollen Dustlike substance produced by male sex cells in flowers.

Pollination Transfer of male pollen to female pistils for development of seeds and fruit.

Potash Common name for potassium.

Potassium One of the three key elements for plant growth. Encourages vigor and disease resistance in plants.

Precipitate Insoluble compound formed by a chemical reaction between two or more normally soluble compounds in solution.

Primary Elements Three elements required for plant growth: nitrogen, phosphorus and potassium.

Propagation Growing plants from seed, cuttings, grafting, division or budding.

Pruning Removal of plant parts for the benefit of the remaining parts.

Quicklime Calcium oxide used as a fast acting soil additive to decrease soil acidity.

Rhizome Plant stem that grows horizontally under the soil surface. Iris are grown from rhizomes.

Root or Root Ball Network of roots and soil of a plant when removed from the soil. Usually wrapped in burlap forming a ball.

Root Zone Underground area where a plant's roots are most active. This varies with plants.

Rootbound Plant that has been grown in a container for too long and whose roots form a tightly congested pattern. New growth is impossible until the roots are trimmed and the plant repotted.

Runner Long, slender trailing stems which take root and produce new plants. Strawberries are one example of a plant that grows runners.

Salinity Term used to describe certain soil types with an abundance of chemical salts. Salinity can cause leaves to turn yellow and stunt growth.

Sap Fluids in plants which contain and carry material necessary for plant growth. Sap is moved by pressure from the root system.

Scion Shoot or bud grafted to a rootstock or branch for propagation.

Seedlings First visual evidence of the successful germination of a seed.

Soil Amendment Organic soil additive used to improved drainage, texture, aeration and ability to retain moisture.

Soluble Material that will dissolve in water easily.

Sphagnum Moss-like plant material used for its ability to hold moisture.

Spike Flowering stem along which flowers are directly attached. Gladiolus is an example of a flower spike.

Spore Simple form of reproductive cell. Examples include fungi, algae, mosses and ferns.

Staking Using a stake or rod to support a plant.

Standard Plant that is trained to grow in the shape of a tree although it does not naturally grow this way. A tree rose is an example.

Stolon Stem that creeps along the ground and takes root forming new plants. Strawberry runners are an example of stolons.

Stone Fruit Fruits that have a single pit in the center such as a peach, apricot or plum.

Stress Adverse growing conditions that endanger a plant's health such as lack of water, extreme temperatures or wind.

Sucker In trees, vertical shoot growing from the main branches or rootstock. In tomatoes, any growth that originates at a branch-stem junction.

Subsoil Layer of soil normally found below the layer of the topsoil.

Sulfur Secondary but necessary plant element. It is often used to acidify alkaline soil.

Super Phosphate Fertilizer which contains at least 20% available phosphorus.

Taproot Main root that grows straight down. The root of a dandelion is a good example.

Tender Condition of having a low tolerance to cool weather or freezing temperatures. Tomatoes are tender.

Terminal Bud Bud at the end of a stem.

Thinning For trees, removal of entire branches to open the overall structure of a tree. For plants, removal of some plants to allow growing room for those remaining.

Topdress Surface application of organic material, such as compost, to aid in moisture retention.

Topiary Technique of pruning shrubbery to a shape that resembles animals and geometric figures.

Transpiration Release of moisture from a plant's leaves.

Tropical Plant Plant that originates in tropical regions and which is usually killed by frosts.

Tuber Underground stem from which a plant grows. Similar to rhizomes but shorter. Potatoes are an example of a tuber.

Variety Botanically, a plant that has at least one particular characteristic as well as the general characteristics of the species.

Vine Plant with flexible stems that climb vertically or horizontally with or without support.

Virus Microscopic living particles that can infect plants or insects causing abnormalities or death.

Watershoot In trees, any vertical shoot growing from the main branches or rootstock. In tomatoes, any growth that originates at a branch-stem junction.

Weed Any plant that competes with garden plants for food, water and space. A weed is simply a plant out of place. Controls include physical or chemical removal, or creating conditions depriving the plant of moisture, sunlight or air in which the plant will die on its own.

Index

A Grand Celebration

Grandparents in Poetry

Selected by **Carol G. Hittleman**
and **Daniel R. Hittleman**

Illustrations by **Kay Life**

Wordsong • Boyds Mills Press

To Joel,
     Our special first, on the day you were born
     Our fondest dreams came true.
     We are the proudest of grandparents,
     Having a wonderful grandson like you.

To Garret,
     Second to none, on the day you were born
     We couldn't have asked for more.
     You're an amazing gem in our family,
     Of that you can always be sure.

To Dori,
     Our sweet third, on the day you were born
     Our lives were enriched ever so much.
     A loving granddaughter are you,
     Bringing laughter and joy to every life you touch.

And to all grandchildren who have had the opportunity
to share a very special relationship with a grandparent

—C. G. H. and D. R. H.

Lovingly dedicated to my grandchildren . . .
With thanks to my photographer friends
Emily O'Grady and Bill Gucfa

—K. G. L.

Published by Wordsong
Boyds Mills Press, Inc.
A Highlights Company
815 Church Street
Honesdale, Pennsylvania 18431
Printed in China

U.S. Cataloging-in-Publication Data
(Library of Congress Standards)

A grand celebration : grandparents in poetry / selected by Carol G. Hittleman
and Daniel R. Hittleman ; illustrations by Kay Life.—1st ed.
[32] p. : col. ill. ; cm.
Summary: Laughing and sharing with grandparents in poetry.
ISBN 1-56397-901-2
1. Grandparents—Poetry. 2. Poetry. I. Hittleman, Carol G.
II. Hittleman, Daniel R. III. Life, Kay. IV. Title.
808.819/ 352   21   2002   AC   CIP
2001092232

First edition, 2002
Book designed by Jason Thorne
The text of this book is set in 12-point Palatino.

Visit our Web site at www.boydsmillspress.com

10 9 8 7 6 5 4 3 2 1

Contents

Acknowledgments

Every possible effort has been made to trace the ownership of each poem included in *A Grand Celebration: Grandparents in Poetry*. If any errors or omissions have occurred, corrections will be made in subsequent printings, provided the publisher is notified of their existence.

Permission to reprint copyrighted poems is gratefully acknowledged to the following:

Boyds Mills Press for "Grandmom" from *Toes in My Nose and Other Poems* by Sheree Fitch. Text copyright © 1987 by Sheree Fitch; "Making Pies with Grandfather" from *Baseball, Snakes, and Summer Squash* by Donald Graves. Text copyright © 1996 by Donald Graves; "Storyteller Nana" from *Under the Breadfruit Tree* by Monica Gunning. Text copyright © 1998 by Monica Gunning; and "When" from *Been to Yesterdays: Poems of a Life* by Lee Bennett Hopkins. Text copyright © 1995 by Lee Bennett Hopkins. Published by Boyds Mills Press, Inc. Reprinted by permission.

Children's Book Press for "My Grandma's Songs" from *Laughing Tomatoes and Other Spring Poems* by Francisco X. Alarcón. Copyright © 1997 by Francisco X. Alarcón. Reprinted by permission of Children's Book Press.

Crown Publishers for "Grandfathers Are to Love" from *Grandchildren Are So Much Fun, I Should Have Had Them First* by Lois Wyse. Copyright © 1992 by Garret Press, Inc. Reprinted by permission of Crown Publishers, a division of Random House, Inc.

Curtis Brown, Ltd., for "All Kinds of Grands" by Lucille Clifton. Copyright © 1990 by Lucille Clifton. From *Poems for Grandmothers*, edited by Myra Cohn Livingston, published by Holiday House. Reprinted by permission of Curtis Brown, Ltd.

Dell Publishing for "Grandpa in March" from *Make a Circle Keep Us In* by Arnold Adoff. Copyright © 1975 by Arnold Adoff. Used by permission of Dell Publishing, a division of Random House, Inc.

Dial Books for Young Readers for "Under the Rainbow" by Lucille Clifton. Copyright © 1993 by Lucille Clifton. From *Soul Looks Back in Wonder* by Tom Feelings; and "remembering" from *Something on My Mind* by Nikki Grimes. Copyright © 1978 by Nikki Grimes. Used by permission of Dial Books for Young Readers, a division of Penguin Putnam Inc.

HarperCollins Publishers for "As Soon as She Is Up" from *Greens* by Arnold Adoff; "I look at this picture of that old man" and "Oma was sixty-three when I was born" by Gerald Dumas and "Lineage" by Margaret Walker. From *Grandparents' Houses* by Corrine Streich; "Old Photograph Album: Grandfather" from *Who Shrank My Grandmother's House? Poems of Discovery* by Barbara Juster Esbensen. Copyright © 1992 by Barbara Juster Esbensen; "Pineapple Surprise" from *Hopscotch Love* by Nikki Grimes. Text copyright © 1999 by Nikki Grimes; and "Grandpa McWheeze" and "Hurry Grandma Hurry" from *A Pizza the Size of the Sun* by Jack Prelutsky. Text copyright © 1996 by Jack Prelutsky. Used by permission of HarperCollins Publishers.

Leland B. Jacobs for "What Grandma Says" by B. J. Lee from *Hello, People!* compiled by Leland B. Jacobs, published by Garrard Publishing Co. Copyright © 1972 by Leland B. Jacobs. Used with permission.

Picture Me Books for "My Grandma" from *Picture Me with My Grandma* by Catherine McCafferty, Picture Me Books, copyright © 1998. Used with permission.

Marian Reiner for "Basket" from *Worlds I Know and Other Poems* by Myra Cohn Livingston. Copyright © 1985 by Myra Cohn Livingston. A McElderry Book; and "From Her Office" by R. H. Marks from *Poems for Grandmothers*, edited by Myra Cohn Livingston, published by Holiday House. Copyright © 1990 by R. H. Marks. Used by permission of Marian Reiner.

Scholastic Inc. for "Grandmother" from *Navajo: Visions and Voices Across the Mesa* by Shonto Begay. Copyright © 1995 by Shonto Begay; "Grandpa" from *Relatively Speaking: Poems About Family* by Ralph Fletcher, published by Orchard Books, an imprint of Scholastic, Inc. Copyright © 1999 by Ralph Fletcher. Reprinted by permission of Scholastic Inc.

The relationship between a grandparent and a grandchild can be an extraordinary one, built on the loving bond that develops between them as they spend special times together.

In these poems, grandparents are enjoyed and celebrated, act as sources of family stories, evoke memories, and create deep friendships with their grandchildren. Readers will understand how
• grandparents and grandchildren share a unique, "grand" relationship;
• grandchildren learn family stories and aspects of their culture from their grandparents;
• grandchildren and grandparents laugh together; and
• grandchildren preserve memories of their grandparents.

Readers will surely realize the special family links that come from the important relationship between grandparents and grandchildren.

Family faces are magic mirrors. Looking at people who belong to us, we see the past, present, and future.

—Gail Lunet Buckley

All Kinds of Grands

She
rocks in a chair and
She
walks with a sign
and they're both of them
Grands
and they're both of them
Mine!

She
taught me to knit and
She taught me to dance
and I wouldn't trade either
of them, not a chance!

She
rocks me to sleep and
She shouts me awake
and they both of them love me
and both, for my sake,

do all kinds of grand things
they wouldn't have guessed.
Oh, all kinds of Grands
are the Grands that are best!

—*Lucille Clifton*

Grandmom

My mom's mom is my grandmom
But I just call her Nanny
And Nanny is the neatest granny
Anyone ever had

Nanny knits my mittens
Nanny braids my hair
Nanny smells like violets
Nanny's always there

And Nanny she wears blue jeans
And swings on swings with me
And when I stay at her house
We never watch TV

We look at pictures of my mom
When she was very young
The one I like the best
Is where she's sticking out her tongue

Nanny wears a bracelet
That jingles on her wrist
And whenever Nanny hugs me
She leaves a lipstick kiss

Nanny serves me Kool-Aid
In her finest china cup
I'm going to be just like her
Whenever I grow up

When Nanny tucks me in my bed
We play a game of let's pretend
My nanny is my grandmum
My nanny is my friend

And Nanny is the neatest granny
Anyone ever had.

—Sheree Fitch

Grandfathers Are to Love

Sometime between the time tonight
When you put away your blocks,
And the time tomorrow
When you put on your sox . . .
Someone will be thinking of you.

Oh, probably a lot of someones
Will be thinking about you.
Your mommy and your daddy, of course,
And your aunt in Upsaloosa.
The mailman, the sandman,
And the Tooth Fairy
Will all think of you very
Often.

Still this is a different someone.

This is someone
Who thinks of you
Even when you don't
Think of him.

This is a grandfather.

Grandfathers come in all sizes.
They come tall and short,
Hairy and bald,
Thin and fat.
But more than that—

They come when you call them.

That's what grandfathers are for.

For instance, if you need
A dinosaur gaboo
Grandfather would rush right out
To get it just for you.

And should you feel unhappy
And very, very sad.
Who'd cuddle you close?
Why, your darling granddad.

Have a problem with your pup
Or a small alligator?
Where do you get advice?
From your dear old grandpater.

If you have someone to visit
Far far away—
Like two streets from here—
Gramps would take you to play.

—*Lois Wyse*

Old Photograph Album: Grandfather

I see him one Christmas
in his leather
aviator hat   the flaps
buckled under his
chin   His hand
is holding the rope
of the Flexible Flyer sled
You can tell it is made of wood

It is piled with Christmas presents
all wrapped in black
and white and gray   A black tree
trimmed with fat white
lights
stands on the porch

The skies of his childhood
are gray   Here he is
in his swimming
suit and his waterwings
He is squinting at the gray sun
that blazes down
on small black sailboats   white
sails   and on the gray waves
lapping at the sand

He is a gray child   and his big dog
is dark gray   Even his baby sister
is gray   Her white curls
bob in the wind   and a gray robin
hops
    off the page

—*Barbara Juster Esbensen*

As Soon as She Is Up

Grandma is up
        And
        Out   side
Picking the
Fresh
     And
       New
     And
     Tender

Dandelion greens to
        Cook
         Up
        For
         Us
         All

    —*Arnold Adoff*

Oma was sixty-three when I was born—
No one who knew
Eugenia Herrman Holm, neither child, grandchild, neighbor
Nor acquaintance could find a flaw. Her finely creased face,
Her cheek, the softest and most mystifying I ever kissed,
Her slow, soothing, cracked-mellow voice all invested me
With a deep wonder and deeper calm.
The house reflected her. Serenity, people said, such serenity
In that house. She was the gentlest woman I ever knew,
And those who had known her fifty years or more, they said so too.

—*Gerald Dumas*

grandpa in march

goes   around
        the house
        each
        day

and feels the
      ground
and pinches
          twigs
and   digs
and   digs

pushing
spring

—*Arnold Adoff*

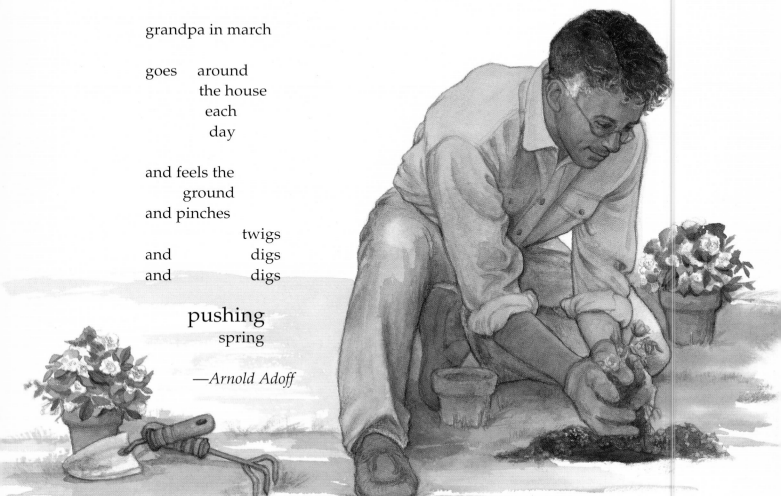

From Her Office

Between her trips she picks up the phone
and calls from her office. She asks can I guess
what she bought me, and won't I come
over tomorrow for lunch

       unless

she has to go off to Chicago again.
But never mind, she loves me a lot,
and did her postcard ever arrive?
And is it possible I forgot

to draw her a picture to hang on her wall?
Her desk is always such a mess.
Somehow she'll get the present to me
and soon she'll have time for lunch

       unless

she has to fly out to Frisco next week—
her other phone's ringing, but don't I know
she thinks of me always, wherever she is
and never forgets, she loves me so.

       —R. H. Marks

*The bond between child and grandparent can indeed be the purest,
least complicated form of human love.*

—Foster W. Cline

Making Pies with Grandfather

Grandfather sings while he works;
his hands move slowly, peeling apples,
rolling dough, sprinkling sugar
and cinnamon until a pie
appears in the kitchen of his restaurant.

"Another bag of sugar, please."
I race to the storeroom
and plop it on the counter.
"My, you're speedy."

He's short of apples
and I get the peeler,
place the apples
on two spikes, turn the crank,
watch the ribbons
of peel drop to the counter.
He laughs, "How did you know
how to use that machine?"

Six apple pies on the counter,
ready for the oven.
"I can't believe we've
made six pies before 7:00 A.M.
'Course, I've never had speedy
help like this before."
He lifts the handle
to the giant oven door,
a blast of hot air
strikes us in the face.
"Put on these mittens;
I think a boy who works so fast
is old enough to put pies in the oven."

—Donald Graves

Basket

Grandmother's basket
of ribbon and lace
is kept in a high-up closet place.

But when I go over
she'll take it out
and let me rummage all about

and find materials.
I can choose
whatever Grandmother doesn't use

when she knits an afghan
or sews a gown.
So whenever I see her take it down

I think of the things
my dolls could wear
of whatever my grandmother has to spare.

—*Myra Cohn Livingston*

Pineapple Surprise

Grandma wasn't much for hugging.
She was entirely too frail
to give me piggyback rides
and moved too slow
for hide-and-seek.
But sometimes,
while I played alone,
she would magically appear
with pineapple upside-down cake,
which took considerable trouble to make:

Honey-glazed pineapple rings
clinging to the bottom—
or was it the top?
Maraschino cherries pop-
ping with tooth tingling
tangy sweetness,
two thick layers of buttery,
gooey, scrumptiously chewy,
pineapple-licious yellow cake
baked for nobody else but me.

—Nikki Grimes

Storyteller Nana

I think of Nana
sitting by the fireside,
cooking and humming calypso tunes;
me, on the hardened earth by her side.

"Tell me a story, Nana," I beg.
Her eyes light up like fireflies
and tales of Brer Anansi
flow from her lips.

When Nana tells her stories
it sounds as if she's reading.
No one would ever guess
she never learned to read a book.

—*Monica Gunning*

Grandpa

When the leaves turn colors
Grandpa comes to visit
and we go hunting arrowheads.

Did you know that your ancestors were archers,
makers of fine bows and arrows?
It's true, you know.

They fitted feathers onto their arrows
to make them fly straight
and strike true.

I tell him archery is pretty cool
but I want to be a writer
when I grow up.

Well then, he says, *what feathers will you use*
to make your words fly
straight and true?

—Ralph Fletcher

My Grandma

I love to visit Grandma
When it's just us two.
She always has a hug for me
And fun things to do.

We start out in the garden
Where we pull the weeds.
When I pull flowers by mistake,
We just plant new seeds!

We cool off with lemonade,
And make sweet cookies, too.
We stir and bake, then sit and take
Some time to eat a few!

Then Grandma gets out the storybooks
For my favorite part of the day.
She reads and I turn pages.
I like sharing stories that way!

I really love my Grandma,
And I know she loves me, too.
I can't wait for my next visit,
Another day of just-us-two!

—Catherine McCafferty

Grandparents are for wondering with you.
—Charlie W. Shedd

Grandpa Dropped His Glasses

Grandpa dropped his glasses once
In a pot of dye,
And when he put them on again
He saw a purple sky.
Purple birds were rising up
From a purple hill,
Men were grinding purple cider
At a purple mill.
Purple Adeline was playing
With a purple doll,
Little purple dragonflies
Were crawling up the wall.
And at the supper table
He got crazy as a loon
From eating purple apple dumplings
With a purple spoon.

—Leroy F. Jackson

What Grandma Says

When I wiggle,
When I squirm,
Father says
I'm like a worm.
But grandma says
That isn't true.
I'm doing what
A child must do.

When it's bedtime
And I scowl,
Mother says
I'm like an owl.
But grandma says
It isn't true.
I'm doing what
Most children do.

—*B. J. Lee*

My Wise Old Grandpapa

When I was but a little chap
My grandpapa said to me,
"You'll need to know your manners, son,
When you go out to tea.

"Remove the shells from hard-boiled eggs,
Make sure your hat's on straight,
Pour lots of honey on your peas
To keep them on the plate.

"Blow daintily upon your tea
To cool it to your taste,
And always pick bones thoroughly,
With due regard for waste.

"Be heedful of your partners' needs,
Attend their every wish;
When passing jelly, cream or jam,
Make sure they're in the dish.

"When eating figs or coconuts,
To show you are refined,
Genteelly gnaw the centers out
And throw away the rind.

"If you should accidentally gulp
Some coffee while it's hot,
Just raise the lid politely and
Replace it in the pot.

"Don't butter ice cream when it's warm,
Or drink soup through a straw."
Thus spoke my wise old grandpapa
When I was only four.

—*Wilbur G. Howcroft*

Grandpa McWheeze

I'm Grandpa McWheeze,
and I do as I please,
I'm quite a remarkable fellow.
I stand on my head
while I butter my bread,
or paint my rhinoceros yellow.

I'm building a boat
I've designed not to float,
I frequently read in the shower.
I play two bassoons
that I fashioned from prunes,
I tango in barrels of flour.

I'm Grandpa McWheeze,
I tie springs to my knees,
I live in a hollow old tree.
I wear snakes on my neck,
and I sort of suspect
there are very few grandpas like me.

—Jack Prelutsky

24

Hurry Grandma Hurry

Hurry Grandma hurry,
Grandma look at me,
I'm right side up, I'm upside down,
I'm swinging from a tree.
I'm jumping like a squirrel,
I think that I can fly—
Grandma please don't worry,
Grandma please don't cry.

Hurry Grandma hurry,
see what I can do,
I'm roller-skating backwards
across the avenue.
Here's a luscious little bug,
I think I'll take a bite—
Grandma stop your screaming,
everything's all right.

Hurry Grandma hurry,
Grandma watch me please,
I'm climbing up a ladder,
I'm dangling by my knees.
I found this giant spider
that was stuck in globs of paint,
Grandma take a closer look—
whatever made you faint?

—*Jack Prelutsky*

If the very old will remember, the very young will listen.
—Chief Dan George

remembering
Grandma filling up this porch
with laughing
and stories about when
Mama was a little girl
and Grandma would hug me
and say
I was her very special own granddaughter.
But now she's gone.
I miss her —

—Nikki Grimes

Under the Rainbow

I close my eyes
and slide along the arc
to home where my long grandmothers
sleep, dreaming of me,
dreaming of how dark
and beautiful we are together
under the bright
rainbow of our nights.

—Lucille Clifton

Lineage

My grandmothers were strong.
They followed plows and bent to toil.
They moved through fields sowing seed.
They touched earth and grain grew.
They were full of sturdiness and singing.
My grandmothers were strong.

My grandmothers are full of memories
Smelling of soap and onions and wet clay
With veins rolling roughly over quick hands
They have many clean words to say.
My grandmothers were strong.
Why am I not as they?

—*Margaret Walker*

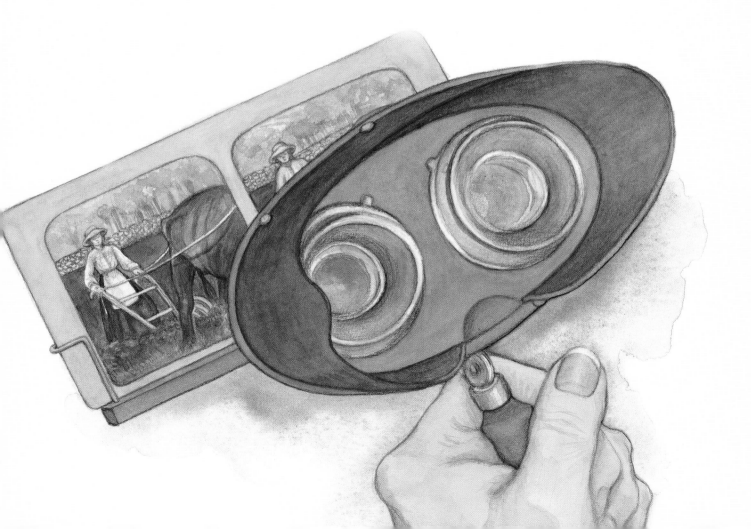

Grandmother

Grandmother was strong, like a distant mesa.
From her sprang many stories of days long ago.
From her gentle manners
lessons were learned
not easily forgotten.
She told us time and again
that the earth is our mother,
our holy mother.

"Always greet the coming day
by greeting your grandparents,
Yá' át' ééh Shi cheii (Hello, My Grandfather)
to the young juniper tree.
Yá' át' ééh Shi másání (Hello, My Grandmother)
to the young piñon tree."

The lines in her face were marks of honor,
countless winters gazing into the blizzard,
many summers in the hot cornfield.
Her strong brown hands, once smooth,
carried many generations,
gestured many stories,
wiped away many tears.
The whiteness of her windblown hair,
a halo against the setting sun.

My grandmother was called Asdzán Ałts'íísí,
Small Woman. Wife of Little Hat,
mother of generations of Bitter Water Clan,
she lived 113 years.

—*Shonto Begay*

When

I was young,
before
I went
to bed,
a nursery rhyme
that Grandma
read
each night
still
echoes
through
my head:

When I was just a little he,
My Grandma took me on her knee.
Her smiles and kisses gave me joy
Each time she called me "Darling Boy."

But
now
there's
no more
little he

no more
sitting on
Grandma's knee

no more
smiles
or kisses
or joy

no more
darling

no more
boy.

—*Lee Bennett Hopkins*

My Grandma's Songs

would follow
the beat of
the washing machine

turning
our kitchen
into a dance floor

consoling
the chairs placed
upside down

delighting
the family portraits
on the walls

putting to sleep
the sheets
on the clothesline

giving flavor
to the boiling pot
of beans

the songs
my grandma
used to sing

could make
the stars
come out

could turn
my grandma
into a young girl

going back
to the river
for water

and make her
laugh and cry
at the same time

—Francisco X. Alarcón

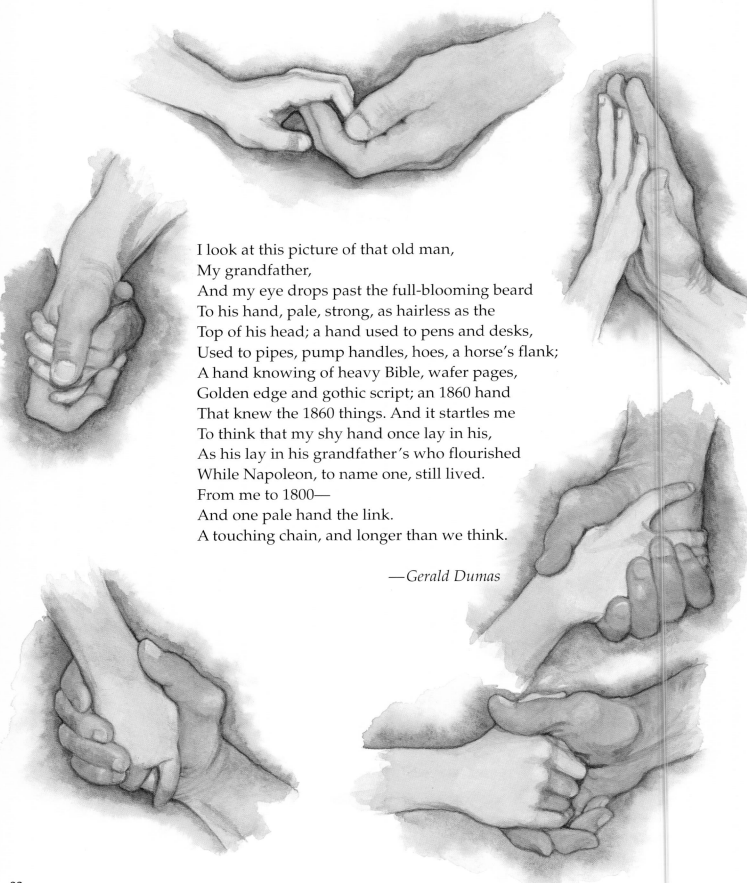

I look at this picture of that old man,
My grandfather,
And my eye drops past the full-blooming beard
To his hand, pale, strong, as hairless as the
Top of his head; a hand used to pens and desks,
Used to pipes, pump handles, hoes, a horse's flank;
A hand knowing of heavy Bible, wafer pages,
Golden edge and gothic script; an 1860 hand
That knew the 1860 things. And it startles me
To think that my shy hand once lay in his,
As his lay in his grandfather's who flourished
While Napoleon, to name one, still lived.
From me to 1800—
And one pale hand the link.
A touching chain, and longer than we think.

—*Gerald Dumas*